"The thrust of Ed Stetzer and Philip Nation's *Compelled* is an argument for hope that the ultimate call on each of our lives—especially as church leaders—is neither to success, contemporary savvy, media or Internet slickness, or admin or business acumen. Since the spirit of love—woven into every action and attitude—is thus the ultimate standard by which our persons and pursuits will be evaluated, Ed and Philip's multilevel elaboration of our various ministry focuses affords a heart-searching, scripturally solid means for truly measuring our ministry efforts in the Father's eyes."

—*Jack W. Hayford, chancellor, The King's University—Los Angeles*

"*Compelled* . . . a compelling resource to spur conversation in small groups."

—*Bill Easum, cofounder, Easum, Bandy & Associates.*

"Ed and Philip talk about the ultimate purpose of missions—to first love God with all our heart, and then to love others as we love ourselves. Love trumps mission, and together they equal missional love."

—*Elmer Towns, dean, School of Religion, Liberty University*

"It is due largely to the church's near systemic failure in discipleship that after 2,000 years of Christianity we still need books on missionality to keep our hearts burning for Jesus and our minds focused on His purposes in the world. We still need expert guidance on the topic. Thankfully, Ed and Philip are about as good guides as you will find anywhere. A worthy read!"

—*Alan Hirsch, author of numerous award-winning books on missional discipleship, including* Untamed *and* Right Here, Right Now

"Too often church leaders portray the mission of the church as a formula. Not so in *Compelled*. Through story and real-life application, Ed and Phillip proclaim that love propels us back to the simple truth: Experiencing God's sacrificial love propels us out into the world—not with a formula—but with the vitality of his saving love. ."

—*The Rev. Canon William Beasley, www.greenhousemovement.com*

"*Compelled* is a much-needed *Start Here!* sign for missional ministry. That's because love is the fuel—not an additive—for serious Christ-followers and churches. Fulfilling the Great Commission (i.e., making Christlike disciples) does not begin with better techniques, strategies, branding, social action, or technology. It begins with our lives being captivated by the Great Commandment (that is, loving God and loving others wholeheartedly). This personal pursuit of "perfect love" has inspired great revivals in the past. It is the essential starting point from which we must set out to lead people, communities, and nations toward spiritual transformation today. Get ready to respond to what the Holy Spirit wants to say to you through this amazing book.

—*Jerry Pence, General Superintendent, The Wesle*

Also by Stetzer & Nation

Ed Stetzer, executive editor
Philip Nation, general editor

ED STETZER
&
PHILIP NATION

COMPELLED

LIVING THE
MISSION OF GOD

NEW HOPE
PUBLISHERS

Birmingham, Alabama

New Hope® Publishers
P. O. Box 12065
Birmingham, AL 35202-2065
newhopedigital.com

New Hope Publishers is a division of WMU®.

The Library of Congress has cataloged an earlier edition as follows:

Stetzer, Ed.
   Compelled by love : the most excellent way to missional living/Ed Stetzer and Philip Nation.
      p. cm.
   Includes bibliographical references.
   ISBN-13: 978-1-59669-227-5 (sc)
   ISBN-10: 1-59669-227-8 (sc)
1. Bible. N.T. Corinthians, 2nd, V, 14-15--Criticism, interpretation, etc. 2. Love--Biblical teaching. I. Nation, Philip, 1970- II. Title.
BS2675.6.L6S74 2008
241'.4--dc22
                              2008000060

ISBN-10: 1-59669-351-7
ISBN-13: 978-1-59669-351-7
N124104 • 0612 • 5M1

Cover and interior design: Michel Lê

To my wife, Angie:

for being the living proof that boundless love and joy
are possible in this life

—*Philip Nation*

To Donna:

who taught me more about showing love than I could learn
in a million books

—*Ed Stetzer*

Contents

PART I—DEATH BY LOVE: GOD AND MISSION

PART II—IDENTIFYING LOVE: THE CHURCH IN THE WORLD

PART III—FORMED BY LOVE: BELIEVERS AND THE WORLD

PREFACE

In 2008, New Hope Publishers asked me to coauthor a book about one of the great underlying reasons for *missional* living: love. I asked Philip Nation to join me as coauthor, and our book became: *Compelled by Love.*

Compelled is a substantive revision of that previous work. This revision occurred as Philip and I served respectively as general and executive editor of *The Mission of God Study Bible* (HCSB). We will use that Bible as the primary version of Scripture for this book and encourage you to use the Bible as your primary guide for understanding God's mission.

Philip and I desire to help all Christians act on God's call to live and proclaim the gospel. We hope this book serves as a continuing encouragement, reminder, and, when necessary, a work to provoke believers to find every way possible to engage in God's mission for His church.

As you use this book, and as you access additional study material in *The Mission of God Study Bible*—from pastors, church planters, vocational missionaries, and other church leaders—we hope that you will both learn and live out God's love by Christ.

As a *missiologist*, meaning I study culture to help pastors and churches reach people for Christ, I teach Christians to see themselves as though they live in a missionary setting. Even if they never leave their neighborhoods. I work to help believers understand what it means to have a *missional* lifestyle: every day we encounter people who need to know Jesus; and if we think like missionaries, then we're more likely to reach them.

Philip Nation is not only my coauthor. Philip and I have worked together as pastors in two churches; and because of that, I know Philip is also an excellent model of this book's principles.

He models Christlike leadership in his home and his church. He has also modeled that love as a pastor, when on staff at a megachurch, and as a church planter. He approaches work in the church not as a professional but as a person who simply wants to live the love of Christ for others. Philip's willingness to coauthor this book is one reason I wrote, and he's a huge part of this book.

Having said that, we decided it would help you as a reader to know when I or Philip or both of us are speaking. I write as the lead author in first person and refer to Philip's references (as in this sentence). Yet, please know that when the book says "I," it most often means "we."

Our Theme

The theme of this book is simple: the love of Christ should compel believers to live out the mission of God (2 Corinthians 5:14–15). And as God's love compels us, He also will change everything about us. The three simple words found in 1 John 4:8 remind us that *God is love*. If we intend to live out a missional calling—an assignment from Christ that all believers are on mission for Him in this world (Matthew 28:18–20)—then it would make sense that our success in this assignment requires us to come into a closer communion with God (Matthew 22:37). If we are going to live a life characterized by His presence and the transformation He affects in our lives, His love ought to compel us. After all, He *is* love.

How to Use *Compelled*

We've structured this book in a way that it can be used best in groups, though you also can use it as an individual. If you are not working through the book in a group, take time to think through the topics and questions for personal reflection. As you will discover—for the first time or again—our faith is not lived out in a vacuum. It beckons for a community aiding one another to integrate love into all aspects of our missional calling. You might consider reading a chapter at a time and then discussing it with others. The points at the end of each chapter will help with that process.

Our Prayer

Our prayer is that God will use *Compelled: Living the Mission of God* to help transform your thinking and actions. As we have had this privilege to write of Christ's love, we hope you will feel His compelling call to carry the gospel into your mission fields of family, neighborhoods, and communities. We hope the nations will be glad that Christ's love has called you into His service.

ACKNOWLEDGMENTS

Thanks to Jeff Clark, Dino Senesi, Larry Bull, and Jon Walker for their help. Thanks also to the churches where we currently serve as teaching pastors; Grace Church (Ed) and The Fellowship (Philip).

Chapter 1

COMPELLED BY LOVE

THE MOST EXCELLENT WAY

"FOR CHRIST'S LOVE COMPELS US."

—2 CORINTHIANS 5:14

N othing you could say or offer could make me do what I was about to do. No argument could persuade me; no threat could pressure me. Yet I was about to do it, voluntarily. Why on earth would I be compelled to do this? What was going on inside me? Then a simple and clear question formed in my head: *Could this be love?* Could it be that love was the force, the energy, the compelling drive that urged me to do something that repulsed me—and would no doubt repulse you?

Love? I have to tell you that, as a kid, I gave up on love. Seriously! You can track it straight to the third grade when I decided that "love" was for girls. My parents thought it was funny, but I wasn't kidding. From the third grade through high school, I signed all my greeting cards, not with the usual "Love, Ed," but with "From, Ed"—just to make my point.

It's probably not surprising that I'd feel this way. I was raised in an Irish family, and we said "I love you" only once a year, *whether we needed to or not.* We had, basically, two emotions in my family: drunk and sleepy; so love wasn't on our short list of feelings.

But now, as I was about to do this gross and disgusting deed, I thought, *So this is love? I am compelled to do this because I love my daughter.* Of course, all of these thoughts flashed through my mind in a millisecond, as I cupped my hands and caught my daughter's vomit so she would not get it all over herself. Instead of following my natural instinct to jump out of the way, love for my little girl compelled me to stay right by her side, letting her know she was not alone and everything was OK. In that moment, I knew something inside me had changed.

The Apostle Paul never specifically said compelling love means catching vomit in your hands, but he did teach that *this* love will characterize our lives and ministries as it becomes the core motivation and driving force of all we do: *"For Christ's love compels us"* (2 Corinthians 5:14). Paul's words tell us that, as we receive the love of Christ in our lives, we'll willingly let it change the way we live. It will change the very way that we think and act. The love of Christ influences every decision we make. His love becomes our way of life and *not mere emotion.*

A lesser love than God's

It's easy to buy into love as mere emotion, like in the popular romantic comedy movies of our day: boy meets girl, boy and girl fall in love, boy loses girl, boy comes to his senses (because it's always his fault!), boy and girl find each other again to live happily ever after—or at least until the sequel. This Hollywoodization of love is so pervasive that many of us, including many Christians, have reduced love to the feel-good emotions of romance, marriage, sex; and not necessarily in that order. Certainly, romance, marriage, and even the physical intimacy between spouses are a part of love, but they are not the full expression of love that's essential to God's nature (1 John 4:16).

Most notably, *God's love includes sacrifice*; in fact, the two—love and sacrifice—cannot be separated. God's version of compelling love intertwines Christ's love with Christ's death:

For Christ's love compels us, since we have reached this conclusion: if One died for all, then all died. And He died for all so that those who live should no longer live for themselves, but for the One who died for them and was raised.

—2 CORINTHIANS 5:14–15

Through His sacrificial love, God brings us into an intimate relationship with Him through salvation. He then compels us to love others as Christ loved us—*first*. Sacrifice on behalf of others is not for the weak and not likely seen apart from love. The love Paul speaks of is born of a strength and resilience that challenges us to live for others, even for those too weak and feeble to give anything back to us. It's a love that challenges us to follow God Himself—the Commander of heaven—and to imitate His sacrifice as we serve others on His behalf: *"We cared so much for you that we were pleased to share with you not only the gospel of God but also our own lives, because you had become dear to us"* (1 Thessalonians 2:8).

Most of all, it is a courageous love that storms the gates of hell and persists beyond the grave. The power of a love that extends even beyond death is a central theme to a particularly clever movie, *The Princess Bride*. After a long period of thinking, pirates killed her true love, Westley, the innocent and lovely Buttercup discovers he's not dead. Yet in the intervening time, the evil Prince Humperdinck has forced her into an engagement.

Upon the bid to rescue her, Westley asks Buttercup why she didn't wait for him to return, and she replies that she thought he was gone forever or, even worse, dead. His reply is classic: "Death cannot stop true love. All it can do is delay it for a while." God's love cannot be stopped by death; in fact, it is in the death and resurrection of Jesus Christ that we see the power of His love.

We display our love through actions

It is a foundational truth for all Christians—Christ's love compels us to display love through our actions: "*We cared so much for you that we were pleased to share with you not only the gospel of God but also our own lives, because you had become dear to us*" (1 Thessalonians 2:8).

Paul says we're compelled by this love in order to persuade others to the gospel, which is a key purpose of the missional life. He wrote to the believers in Corinth:

> *Therefore, because we know the fear of the Lord, we seek to persuade people. We are completely open before God, and I hope we are completely open to your consciences as well. We are not commending ourselves to you again, but giving you an opportunity to be proud of us, so that you may have a reply for those who take pride in the outward appearance rather than in the heart.*
> *For if we are out of our mind, it is for God;*
> *if we have a sound mind, it is for you.*
>
> —2 CORINTHIANS 5:11–13

The Message paraphrase renders verse 13 as, "*If I acted crazy, I did it for God; if I acted overly serious, I did it for you.*" Paul's point is that his actions are birthed from a deep love for *both* God and the church. Our work of persuasion, which is birthed by love, results in an externally focused life. Why do we work to persuade people of the truth? Because God loves them and compels us to do the same.

Christ's love compels and convinces us that He died for people everywhere. Martin Luther (the revolutionary monk who began the Protestant Reformation) called John 3:16 "the gospel in miniature": *For God so loved the world, that he gave his only begotten Son, that whosoever believeth in him should not perish, but have everlasting life*" (KJV). This was once the most quoted verse of the Bible in America. That is no longer the case. Today in North American culture, it seems Matthew 7:1 is the most quoted verse in the whole Bible: *Judge not, that ye be not judged*" (KJV). This is a culture waiting to be embraced by love. The only compelling and convicting foundation for the believer to meet this need is the sufficient death of Christ for sin.

God loved the world in such a way that He did something. What an important fact for us to remember! We should focus on the difference occurring by what we do—a difference created by the presence of Christ's love and what that love accomplished for us. As Philip and I began work on the study notes for *The Mission of God Study Bible*, we did so for the specific purpose of helping people better understand God's work in the world. It is my prayer that such a project will help all believers engage in all of God's mission.

A few years ago, I sat down with my family to have a devotional time at the kitchen table. As you might know, devotions with an eight-year-old, a five-year-old, and a two-year-old are . . . challenging. On this particular night, we read the story of Zacchaeus. It is devotional gold for kids: a short guy who wants to see Jesus, climbing in a tree, Jesus telling him to come down, immediate obedience, hanging around with lost people, and witnessing.

Knowing Zacchaeus's story is packed with kid-friendly lessons, I began to question my children about the story. It only took two responses to realize that one child was hungry and the other only wanted to know what a sycamore tree was. Very quickly, the devotional became wearisome. But why do we continue, even when the right result isn't visible? Christ's love compels us! We want our children to be as convinced as we are that One died for all because of Christ's love. So I try to persuade my hungry and curious children.

Romans 4:7–8 gives further understanding of our key passage: *"How joyful are those whose lawless acts are forgiven and whose sins are covered! How joyful is the man the Lord will never charge with sin!"* Here, Paul was quoting Psalm 32:1–2. We see why it matters that one died for all: Sins are covered, and the sinner is no longer charged with sin! God's love goes beyond forgiveness of sin; He removes, from our permanent record, the charges against us.

Living as love

Consider the marriage relationship. When a woman and man marry, they each choose to live differently because they now live for one another. The spouse's needs take on more meaning than his or her own because of love and commitment.

As Christians, we are called to restructure our lives around a loving God. We change because of our redemption. If change does not occur, we evaluate whether we have truly passed from death to life or have merely taken on ourselves the social descriptor of "Christian." Many people *claim* to be Christian, but they are miserable, unhappy, and ungracious.

Intimacy with Christ and experiencing His compelling love should convince us of the truth that our lives are surrendered to His redemption and our behavior is changed. Something is wrong when churches are known as places of conflict rather than Christlikeness, as places of gossip rather than exhortation, or as places of exclusion rather than havens of love.

God's Word teaches us this about the Christian's life progression:

For through the law I have died to the law, so that I might live for God. I have been crucified with Christ and I no longer live, but Christ lives in me. The life I now live in the body, I live by faith in the Son of God, who loved me and gave Himself for me.

—GALATIANS 2:19–20

Crucifixion is not crossing over a line, realizing your best life now, or finding a Zen moment in the midst of conflict. Crucifixion of self is love and death bound together. It is love so compelling that God in the flesh died for humanity. My life is different because the Son of God who loved me gave up His very life. Note the progression again:

> Christ's love in me compels me.
> Christ's love for me convinces me.
> Christ's love at work in me changes me.

When this expression is lived out correctly, Galatians 2:19—*"I have been crucified with Christ"*—becomes the reality of the manner in which we live.

Believers must no longer think lightly or speak glibly about crucifixion. It's not "Quick! Be a good follower of Jesus and give up your media intake for a day. Die to your wants." No, it's painful. It's a battle. It's dramatic. This is the portrait painted by Paul. To the believer, death occurs not only for Christ, but for self as well. The old nature must die so Christ can live in and through us.

We cannot by our own strength be loving persons as Christians. We can only become those persons when Christ lives in us. The change that occurs by Christ's love is the only way we can love *as God loves*. God gives the gracious endowment of the sacrificial life of Christ to indwell us so we might live by faith and not by sight, emotion, or any other earthly power. Once again, we see it all bound together: life, death, and love. *It is death by love.*

Before *The Passion of the Christ* movie in 2004, the typical film portrayed Jesus as a wimpy kind of guy. The 1970s movies portrayed Him as a blue-eyed hippie in a dress, wandering through Israel saying strange things to people, who then began to sing songs and dance—a reflection of that decade. But the Bible focuses on Jesus' strength and determination to fulfill the mission the Father gave Him.

Christ was the Lamb of God, but He wasn't remotely sheepish. *Love* is being crucified with Christ—who also is the Lion of the tribe of Judah. Our crucifixion with Christ is because *"the life I now live in the flesh, I live by faith in the Son of God, who loved me and gave Himself for me."*

Seeing through God's eyes

Second Corinthians 5:14–21 gives us the perspective Paul had for ministry and mission—he indicated he was compelled by love. He wrote this letter to a struggling church that was living out its faith in the midst of a corrupt society. Yet regardless of the circumstances present in the cultural fabric of Corinth, Paul called the church there to engage them with the gospel. What he said he was (*compelled*) is what he taught them to be in the subsequent verses. As such, we think Paul's self-description is worthy of our attention—and our imitation. We, too, are compelled by love.

The teaching drives us to see others through God's eyes. The passage makes clear our role of bringing others to God through Christ:

From now on, then, we do not know anyone in a purely human way. Even if we have known Christ in a purely human way, yet now we no longer know Him in this way. Therefore, if anyone is in Christ, he is a new creation; old things have passed away, and look, new things have come. Everything is from God, who reconciled us to Himself through Christ and gave us the ministry of reconciliation: That is, in Christ, God was reconciling the world to Himself, not counting their trespasses against them, and He has committed the message of reconciliation to us. Therefore, we are ambassadors for Christ, certain that God is appealing through us. We plead on Christ's behalf, "Be reconciled to God." He made the One who did not know sin to be sin for us, so that we might become the righteousness of God in Him.

—2 CORINTHIANS 5:16–21

In one of the final scenes of the movie *Bruce Almighty*, Bruce is hit by a car and meets God in heaven. Up to this point, Bruce has been horribly self-centered, doubted the need for God's providential intervention, and has been particularly bad at prayer. But the final scene is a touching one in which he makes a few jokes with God and God jokes back. Ultimately, God wants Bruce to make a decision about what he wants for his girlfriend, Grace. Their brief interaction goes like this:

God: Grace. You want her back?

Bruce: No. I want her to be happy, no matter what that means. I want her to find someone who will treat her with all the love she deserved from me. I want her to meet someone who will see her always as I do now, through Your eyes.

God: Now *that's* a prayer.

Can you believe it? The Jim Carrey/Morgan Freeman comedy got it! God's call on our lives should cause us to live differently—and to *perceive* life differently. The Scriptures say *"we do not know anyone in a purely human way"* (2 Corinthians 5:16). Being compelled by love means we see people through God's eyes, as God sees them.

Honestly, this can be difficult, and without the Spirit's help, it never gets easier. In crowded malls, we see people as annoyances. At work, some become the enemy. In commuting, they can degenerate to the status of imbecile. Churches lose members (or even split) because of broken relationships. Whenever we perceive others as pests or pains, we are not viewing people as God does. It is a sin when we see people incorrectly. The Scriptures say that from now on we regard no one from a worldly point of view but through God's eyes.

Second Corinthians 5:16 tells us we must also see Christ through a new perspective. We come to know Him for His true nature—the fully divine Messiah who is God in the flesh.

After the declaration of seeing people through God's eyes and how He compels us to love, Paul reminds us in verses 17–19 that, as believers, Jesus doesn't count our sins against us. One significant expression of love is that we stop counting people's sins. It is by seeing them, instead, through God's redeeming view that love breaks forth.

Once Paul taught the Corinthians how they should view others differently, he called all to serve as Christ's ambassadors (vv. 18–20). Once-blind sinners who previously camped outside the kingdom of God are given power and privilege, commissioned as ministers and ambassadors on behalf of the King Himself.

Ambassadors are high-ranking diplomatic officials used to establish good relations between two political powers. The design of the role is to bring about good will between distinct sovereignties with the intent of eventually working together.

Interestingly, in the days of the New Testament, Rome did not send out ambassadors. They did not have to. Rome sent out conquering armies with governors who ruled over the conquered nation. Rome established its authority with neighboring nations not by good will but by overwhelming power.

Other countries sent ambassadors to Rome. They would arrive from as far away as India, entreating the Roman emperor to have mercy. The plea of the visiting ambassador was for Rome to show mercy, to not send an army. The ambassadors would arrive with the message: "Let us be an ally, a vassal state on the border, on the edge of the empire. Let us live." As the weaker states, their only options were to be conquered or to negotiate a surrender.

The all-powerful Roman Empire wouldn't send out ambassadors to those that didn't matter; but the all-powerful, loving, good, sovereign, perfect, and merciful God says that we're ambassadors for Christ, the king of a far greater kingdom. So this glorious, all-powerful God sends ambassadors on his behalf. It is a glorious scheme that confounds the wisdom of this world.

History tells us of some who were great ambassadors and others who were truly poor ambassadors. Ambassadors who anger the people among whom they live can cause wars. As believers, we must take care that we don't cause others to adopt a warlike mentality toward God. We are called to love as God loves.

This better way—the call to love—causes us to be ambassadors who bring a sense of peace. Humans' rebellion is the root cause of our eternal conflict with God. The Bible says all are under God's judgment. Because of that judgment, God gives us the message of reconciliation and sends us out as ambassadors; He makes His appeal for peace through us. Through His offer, our friends can be brought under the rule of God in His kingdom.

Becoming better "lovers"

We would all agree: Christians ought to be the most loving people in the world—but we aren't. Let's face it, churches would be overflowing if we didn't have the reputation of being hypocrites, liars, and so on. Unfortunately, a LifeWay Research study from 2008 found that 72 percent of Americans surveyed believe that the church is filled with hypocrites.[1] But that does not mean we should just throw up our hands and surrender. Nor does it mean that we stop talking about the gospel because it might offend some. If anything, we need to do more to proclaim and demonstrate the gospel by our words and deeds.

As people who have led churches and church plants, we have discovered for ourselves that the lost are waiting to meet the believers who *look like* Jesus, not just *talk about* Him. The book *Jim and Casper Go to Church* tells the story of two journalists who travel the country visiting influential churches. The book reveals Casper, the atheist of the pair, is waiting for the leaders of the church to tell believers what Jesus requires of them. It would seem, from that perspective, Casper isn't searching for the *beliefs* of believers but the *outworking* of those beliefs that will convince him they are true.[2] That attitude is an illustration of the biblical teaching that the world will know we are Christians by our love.

We are changed by Christ's love

We cannot be loving and live for self. Love does not operate selfishly. Love changes us. *"And He died for all so that those who live should no longer live for themselves, but for the One who died for them and was raised"* (2 Corinthians 5:15).

The enormity of God's forgiveness compels us to live differently. Since the God of the universe has treated us in a most loving and forgiving way, Christians should be the most loving and forgiving people on earth. When we fail, we dishonor the One to whom we belong.

Christians and unbelievers alike share the sin of hypocrisy, but we are without excuse because we know better. As unsaved sinners, they are simply living in the way that comes naturally. But when we claim allegiance to the King of kings and Lord of lords, who died on the Cross as the outworking and fulfillment of His love and forgiveness, then we should not act in unloving ways. Something is wrong when a person claims to belong to Christ and yet fails to love others.

Barriers to love

Christ's love compels us, convinces us, and changes us. Not only does God compel us with love and convince us with truth, He indwells us so He can make His appeal through us to the lost of this world—to a spouse, our children, neighbor, co-worker, and friend. The indwelling life of Christ manifests itself through the way we live and the way we love. *"We plead on Christ's behalf, 'Be reconciled to God.' He made the One who did not know sin to be sin for us, so that we might become the righteousness of God in Him"* (2 Corinthians 5:20–21).

Philip and I grew up in diverse environments: he lived in Alabama, and I grew up in New York. My family was culturally Catholic; Philip's family has always been active in a Baptist church. Yet we have one thing in common: sometimes we both struggle with how to be more loving. With all our background differences, our greatest common struggle is whether or not we love people well. The necessity of every missional Christian is to love because of Christ's love within us.

It remains hard to live the Jesus way, to live and love in a way that brings God glory. The power of our flesh cries out for us to be selfish and to refuse to love those who have not treated us well, have worked against our better interest, or have simply been the annoying gnat in our conversation. It turns out that the greatest barrier to love is self.

We are called to be like Ruth in the Old Testament. When faced with a choice to go her own way or care for the grieving Naomi, she stayed. Even though Ruth faced life in a different culture and would be known as an "outsider," her heart was for the need of her mother-in-law. Ruth's heart was in line with the heart of God who cares for the widow in her sorrow. Rather than seek her own comfort or advantage, she set all self-interest aside to care for a woman to whom she owed no debt.

If we operate by our own view of the world and our own strength, we will walk away from people every time. However, Christ's love in us—the conviction of Christ's truth displayed by love and the change in our lives because of redemption—causes us to have a new view of people and a new life of compassion for both the saved and the lost.

APPLICATION CHALLENGE:

Are our lives marked by a compelling love?

As Philip and I write this book on love as the compelling motive, our lives are not always marked by love. The missional mark upon our lives is being changed, renewed, and conformed to look like Christ. As we surrender, we become more like Him. Philip has often said that understanding the missional view of our faith requires a perspective of surrendering, rather than making a treaty.

In a treaty, countries keep their individual sovereignty and trade favors with one another. It is an unacceptable scenario for God. He demands our surrender. We cannot be citizens—much less ambassadors—for a kingdom that does not have our full allegiance.

So one day I made my surrender to the love of Christ because His love, poured out through death and victoriously resurrected by the power of God, compelled and convinced me. Now, I must daily remain a humble ambassador before the Lord to whom I have surrendered. Being convinced and changed by His love, I now am committed to the beautiful work of reconciliation, whereby the sinless One who became sin for us may speak His powerful words of life to the lost and dying around us.

Transforming Power of God's Love

First Corinthians 13 has become most well known as a passage read at marriage ceremonies. It gives us a beautiful picture of love worked out in our lives. But the passage should not be exclusively applied to marriage. The description of love should impact every area of our lives as we live out God's mission.

We should copy God. *"Therefore, be imitators of God, as dearly loved children. And walk in love, as the Messiah also loved us and gave Himself for us, a sacrificial and fragrant offering to God"* (Ephesians 5:1–2). The imitation of God is to serve as a fragrant offering. I'm afraid many of us merely pretend to be an offering. We're great at praising God after a storm has passed, but God calls us to live as children who imitate their loving father, regardless of circumstances.

We are also to walk with God in spite of our past. In John 4, Jesus goes out of His way to meet an anonymous Samaritan woman at a well. Once she is confronted and changed by the presence of Christ, her first impulse is to be missional. She goes into the village where she was most likely an outcast and declares, *"Come, see a man who told me everything I ever did! Could this be the Messiah?"* (John 4:29). And to her delight, they did.

God compels us with love, convinces us with truth, and indwells us so He can speak through us to the lost. This indwelling life of Christ manifests itself through the way we live and the way we love. *"We plead on Christ's behalf, 'Be reconciled to God.' He made the One who did not know sin to be sin for us, so that we might become the righteousness of God in Him"* (2 Corinthians 5:20–21).

The way of Jesus is contrary to what we naturally desire. Our fleshly nature refuses to love those we find unworthy. It's only Christ in us that changes us and makes us see people as God sees them and to live a new life of compassion for both the saved and the lost (see Matthew 22:35–40).

Points for Personal Reflection and Group Discussion

1. In light of the Scriptures regarding *the love of Christ,* how has your understanding of love been changed or challenged?

2. Talk about how properly defining love as the activity of God, instead of an emotional reaction of people, can change the way we approach our lives.

3. Who has God placed in your life recently who needs you to view them from an eternal perspective?

4. Discuss some barriers that keep us from answering God's call to share the message of reconciliation with those around us.

5. After learning the difference between a treaty and a surrender, have you made a treaty with God or have you surrendered to Him? What changes would you like to make?

6. Are you certain Christ's love dwells within you? Take a moment to read through the appendix, "The Path to Salvation," on page 183. Discuss the victory involved with this type of surrender to Christ.

7. As you think of all you have discussed and learned in this session, what is the one thing you will take home and continue to ponder or to seek the power of God's love for change?

**Part I
Death by Love:
God and Mission**

Chapter 2

SEARCHING LOVE

THE FATHER'S HEART FOR US

B eing a parent is something that cannot be fully explained—a mix of joy and frustration; the desire to press children to achieve their full potential but still to be happy in the moment. You serve as the lover of their lives, disciplinarian, spiritual guide—and also should be the source of immense fun.

Philip and I have very different lives. I have three daughters, while Philip has two sons. We have tea parties and go to the American Girl doll store. Philip plays video games and watches football. We both look for the needs our children have and seek to meet them.

It might appeal to you but, I must confess, I'm not a big fan of the American Girl doll store. I don't really have to go to the store, but I love my daughters, so I go and smile. Philip gets stressed trying to teach his teenage son to drive, but they muscle through it. Why would parents, who have total control of their lives (or at least pretend to), subject themselves to activities that are not their favorite thing to do on any particular day? The answer is simple: We love our kids.

We know football games and tea parties may soon be gone from the calendar. But the time spent encouraging, laughing, loving, and guiding will last a lifetime. The *content* of parenting often doesn't seem so important until we see it in the long-term *context* of parenting.

Our heavenly Father is also parenting us with interest in our lives' details—where we go, what we do. The ultimate aim is that we bring glory to Him through properly lived lives. Thus, as we seek to become *missional* believers, it would do us well to better understand our Father's heart toward the church and the world: God searches for us and sends His best.

Missional ministry can only be accomplished provided there is a sure foundation for all we do. We begin with the knowledge of God because the mission originates in His heart. Otherwise, we will find ourselves doing many of the good things possible in this world, but never accomplishing the one *great* thing the kingdom God had in store for us. The work God gives His people rises above mere goodness, because at the heart of who God is, there is a love like none other. Let's look at the character of the Father's love.

Searching Love

All the tax collectors and sinners were approaching to listen to Him. And the Pharisees and scribes were complaining, "This man welcomes sinners and eats with them!" So He told them this parable: "What man among you, who has 100 sheep and loses one of them, does not leave the 99 in the open field and go after the lost one until he finds it? When he has found it, he joyfully puts it on his shoulders, and coming home, he calls his friends and neighbors together, saying to them, 'Rejoice with me, because I have found my lost sheep!' I tell you, in the same way, there will be more joy in heaven over one sinner who repents than over 99 righteous people who don't need repentance.

—LUKE 15:1–7

This is the first portion of perhaps the most well-known parable in the Gospels. For those who grew up going to church, it conjures up memories of flannel board pictures and spontaneous dramas led by Sunday School teachers. But do not be fooled. It is a story about the very nature of God and the heart of His church. It is revolutionary—and offensive to many.

In the context of the passage, we hear the Pharisees' words, dripping with sarcasm about Christ's fraternizing with "sinners." They were scandalized by whom He regarded as His friends. Two thousand years later, we still have that problem. Do we want to do ministry on "that side of town?" Should we really let "those teenagers" go on the retreat? It seems we work hard to insulate ourselves from the very world Jesus says we should be focused on. We have successfully created, without malicious design, a Christian bubble—an evangelical subculture—where Christians live surrounded only by other Christians, and as a result, there are few among the lost whom we get to know intimately.

God's mission is outside the bubble

Christian experts tell us how to raise our kids, how to handle our finances, what music to buy, what movies to see, and which books to read. The bubble is complete. But God is on a mission outside that bubble.

In God, we find the Father, Son, and Spirit who intentionally search for the lost. God purposely goes to those who are far from Him (that's us). He is fully aware of humankind's fall, yet isn't afraid to get His hands dirty. God seeks the lost, and we—in our missional assignment—are to do the same.

In the Luke 15 parable, the shepherd has 99 of his 100 sheep. I suspect many bosses would be happy if an employee had a 99 percent success rate. If you had a year with 99 percent success, the result would be praise, pay raises, promotions, and recognition at the annual retreat—because, after all, *no one* can get it right 100 percent of the time. Right?

The Father stands such conventional wisdom on its head. For the Father, if one sheep is lost, He keeps searching "until . . ."; He doesn't give up. His searching is an "until found" search, not "until tired." It is "until rescued," not "until obligations are fulfilled." It is "until redeemed," not "until conscience is alleviated."

God's searching love is one that ends in joy. Too often we seek only a sense of relief.

Have you ever lost track of a child in a clothing store? I still remember one time when Kristen was playing around and didn't get on the elevator in time. I was on one side of the closing door, and she was on the other. So many images flashed through my mind in those few moments. Panic ensued, followed by yelling, fear, and drama—and once I was done with that, I made a plan.

Kristen had a plan too. She pushed the button, and the door opened. I was still upset, but immensely relieved at the same time.

Have you been there—frantically looking around every clothing rack, up and down the aisles, and in the dressing rooms? Then, when the tyke is found, there is a flood of relief—and a lot of scolding: "You had me so worried. Do you know what could have happened to you? Don't ever walk away from me like that again!"

Love brings back the strays

The Father responds differently when He rescues a stray. He lays the lost lamb across His shoulders. Great care is taken of the lost one. God says, *"I will seek the lost, bring back the strays, bandage the injured, and strengthen the weak, but I will destroy the fat and the strong. I will shepherd them justice"* (Ezekiel 34:16). It isn't a "get-the-job-done" attitude. Someone is lost—wandering off the path by accident; others are strays—intentionally leaving the path in rebellion. Never minding the reason, the Great Shepherd searches for the lamb, bandages its wounds, and works justly.

When Ezekiel wrote this passage, Israel had been disobeying God's command to care for the poor and oppressed. Selfishness overrode the ethic Yahweh had given them. Ezekiel proclaimed that God is seeking strays—the very sheep that were causing a problem. It's the pet you don't want to chase down the road, the child who continually frustrates you, the person you see in the mirror every day (because you know your own sin). But God goes searching, even for the most frustrating strays.

You and I don't find it so hard to see ourselves as lost, stray, weak, and wounded. More often, however, we are something else: We are mutterers. Grumbling and complaining, we want what we do not have. We rebel against the God who has our best interests in mind. Habitually, we are like our children. Even though we despise it in them, we act the same way with God. Yet He searches for us in spite of it. And once the lost sheep is tracked down, He strengthens it and binds its wounds.

Love heals the wounded

The Father does not search just so He can be proud of maintaining a 100 percent record. Rather, His searching love is focused on the goal of healing the wounded. Among those who get lost in the wilderness, injury is common. God is the seeker, the initiator. To quote Philip's friend Henry Blackaby, "God is always at work around you. He is working to bring about world redemption through His Son Jesus Christ."[1]

Before you got up to minister, God was already at work. When you search for a believer gone astray, you are working alongside God Himself. In the middle of proclaiming the gospel to a lost soul, God is pleading His case through you by His loving heart. As you quietly discuss the claims of Christ with someone "far from God," the Father is planting seed in soil He has already tilled. Even if you give up and leave, He is still at work in that life. The Father's searching love is boundless compared to ours.

Our agenda should change. We have a directive from the Lord to not give up on the people around us. He lovingly and persistently pursues them, and we walk with Him in that pursuit.

Jealous Love

Is God jealous? That sounds odd to us, yet the Lord Himself says He holds a jealous love on our behalf.

Genesis tells us the stories of God creating the world and mankind and His choosing of a people for Himself and His glory. It's a magnificent landscape as God's hand reaches out to people—to us. In Exodus, we find God's people in bondage, enslaved with little hope. God chooses a leader: an old man who was once a child of privilege but now is a broken old man guilty of murder. From age 40 to 80, Moses has lived on the back side of the desert, tending sheep that belong to someone else. Eventually, Moses hears the voice of God Himself, calling him to go back to Egypt, where he can be useful to the Lord of hosts. Ultimately, after two tries, God gives Moses and the children of Israel the Ten Commandments. Among them, we find this statement: *"You must not bow down to them or worship them; for I, the LORD your God, am a jealous God, punishing the children for the fathers' sin, to the third and fourth generations of those who hate Me"* (Exodus 20:5).

A member of our church plant asked Philip about this. "I thought jealousy was a sin," she said. "If God is perfect, how can he be jealous?"

In Exodus 34:14, God pushes the idea of jealous love even further: *"You are never to bow down to another god because Yahweh, **being jealous by nature**, is a jealous God"* (emphasis added). This is puzzling, yet revealing of who He is.

As a spouse, I can identify with this characteristic. I am jealous for my wife's affection. This jealousy isn't a sinful jealousy that requires her to be under my control at all times. Rather, I do not want anyone else to harm my mate. I bristle at the idea of another trying to capture my spouse's attention.

Philip officiated at his sister-in-law's wedding. Angie, Philip's wife, was the matron of honor. Philip nearly got in trouble for a terrible oversight.

He explains: "I paid more attention to my wife than I did the bride. The ceremony was held in the same sanctuary in which Angie and I were married 13 years earlier. As Angie came down the aisle in her beautiful dress, all I could remember was the joy of my own wedding day. How could I have that much happiness?

"If you mess with Angie, that's going to be a problem because I am jealous for her love—and for her good. In the Nation household, the greatest offense would be blasphemy. A close second, for my two sons, is to disrespect Mom. I want them to learn a jealous love for the woman who stands at the center of our home."

God's love for us is much greater than the love spouses have for one another. God does not want us distracted. He does not want our loyalties to be divided. Our allegiances are to be His alone. He loves us that intensely.

The question we face is then about our own love. What about that friend who is wayward and lost? What of the one who isn't in the kingdom of God? Do we think, "Someone else will help"; "God will get them eventually"; "I will help them later"?

Do we have the jealous love for others that God has for them?

Paul wrote to the troubled yet triumphant Corinthian church: *"For I am jealous over you with a godly jealousy, because I have promised you in marriage to one husband–to present a pure virgin to Christ"* (2 Corinthians 11:2). The church was at one point rampant with sin. Paul's love, jealous as it was, was helping them return to devotion.

We need to return to the Father's heart regarding our fellow believers. The church is to be presented as a pure virgin. You and I should live in such a way, minister in such a way, that the church gains the benefit. We should desire so deeply that the church remain pure that it reflects in our daily life.

What illustration in all of creation could aptly paint the jealous love of God for us? Husband and wife? Mother for child? What of a warrior battling at the gate for his king? Ultimately, every illustration amounts to nothing more than a mere shadow of the love of God.

On this earth, only Christ Himself can truly portray the jealous love of the Father. Christ's love is so great, He gives Himself up as a sacrifice so hopeless humans can be reunited with the God of light and glory. As we conform to His image, we will live with such a jealous love for our fellow believers too.

Redeeming Love

What is love? God displays and explains it perfectly. Love is not simply a feeling, emotion, or action. Perfect love is redemption. Scripture explains: *"Love consists in this: not that we loved God, but that He loved us and sent His Son to be the propitiation for our sins"* (1 John 4:10). Yes, the Bible says *"God is love"* (1 John 4:8) and that makes a great bumper sticker. It is harder to explain *how* God is love—and the answer to that lies in what God *did*. He showed His love by atoning for our sin.

Through all of Christian history, we have sought to understand God in light of His revelation. We have sought to know the unknowable. Through well-written systematic theologies, we have assigned specific words to describe the nature of God. Great Christians have written and spoken of the work God does to reveal His glory and act on our behalf. But deity cannot be fully defined, and real love is not defined in the ideas about God that we dissect. Our love does not originate from what we have deduced of God and thus love Him out of what we have discovered. Rather, His "first love" overwhelms all our searching for knowledge. He comes to us first and bids us to submit to His love.

The Father's love results in atonement, which means "covering." Christ's atoning sacrifice means our sins are "covered over." His sinlessness covering our sinfulness.

As John wrote, it is also about *propitiation*. The word means *the removal of divine wrath*. When God could have judged us on account of our sin, Christ stands in our place and takes it upon Himself. Instead of seeing our sin, God sees us as His children.

God does not wait for us to become morally pure to bestow salvation upon us. If He did, I could never get there. Now, I'm a relatively moral person. But I can't make myself righteous enough to get to God. Remember, to be a lawbreaker, all I have to do is break one law. When God looks upon us, He sees not our sin but Christ's sacrifice on our behalf. This is how God shows He is love. In Romans 5:8, Paul wrote, *"But God proves His own love for us in that while we were still sinners, Christ died for us!"* The only One who can redeem me is the One who holds perfection within His being—God Himself.

Mankind is greatly blessed that God doesn't wait for us to meet some standard. "Once they get *here*, I will get right down there on earth and save them all." No, He comes to finish a work we can't even pretend to be able to begin.

In hopes of trapping Jesus, the religious elite men of the day brought before Christ a woman they had caught in adultery. (I have often wondered where the man participating in her sin had run off.) But instead of allowing the woman to be stoned by the angry zealots, Jesus reveals the shame of their own sin while offering redemption to her. God offers a relationship to her and sends her away to live righteously. *"Go, and from now on do not sin anymore"* (John 8:11).

In fact, the word for "go" is not the typical Greek word. It carries the emphasis to be on a journey of adherence. Here is a woman others only wanted to use for their own gain, but Christ desired her redemption.

Love comes through our own death

Once we are lovingly called and redeemed by God, our lives change. Often, we are like the Galatians who struggled between rigid legalism and overly applied liberty. Must I be cloistered in a monastery or may I sin all I wish? Neither! Our redemption must be lived out by faith. And a living faith ought to be the result of receiving God's redeeming love. *"I have been crucified with Christ and I no longer live, but Christ lives in me. The life I now live in the body, I live by faith in the Son of God, who loved me and gave Himself for me"* (Galatians 2:19–20). It is not by any work of our own hands, heart, or head. Rather, His redeeming love is my crucifixion as well.

When life crashes, you are laid off from work, spouses spat, rebellious children harbor grudges—it is hard to live by faith. But there is nothing else to live by. All the wisdom of the ages cannot fix the problems we struggle with. No amount of time spent watching talk shows, reading self-help books, or attending personal empowerment conferences can deliver permanent change. But, when we decide, as the old preachers say, "You can't kill a dead man," then our perspective on everything changes. Once we accept our own death in the redeeming love of God, no matter what the world does or anyone throws at me, I live because of Christ.

Rejoicing Love

For as a young man marries a young woman, so your sons will marry you;
and as a groom rejoices over his bride,
so your God will rejoice over you.
—Isaiah 62:5

Donna and I got married when we were 20. (Please don't tell our daughters!) We had been dating since we were 15 years old. She says we started dating when we were 16, but I thought it was 15. I think that makes me a stalker for a whole year!

I remember our wedding well. Few moments can compare with the pure joy felt when the doors of the wedding chapel open and the bride enters. The brightness of her eyes. The crisp white wedding gown. The glow of her smile. It is a moment of elation unlike any other. The joy in her heart is revealed by the lightness in her step as she glides down the aisle toward her groom.

The wedding motif helps us understand the love of God for us. He is joyful over His church as the groom is elated by His bride's entrance. *"Yahweh your God is among you, a warrior who saves. He will rejoice over you with gladness. He will bring you quietness with His love. He will delight in you with shouts of joy"* (Zephaniah 3:17). We are all familiar with the songs of praise to God we sing. Whenever possible, we should sing an extravagant song of adoration, pride, and joy. Though our notes often fall flat, we sing the best we can.

But there is a greater mystery attached to the songs of eternity—God rejoices over *us* with joy. Why? What could you and I possibly do that is worth the breath of the Creator to commit to a shout of joy? Nothing. Absolutely nothing. Yet the same breath that gave us life also delights in declaring joy for our very presence.

The closest comparison we have on earth is when we make up songs for our children. As a father, there is something wonderful when your own child stands in front of you with a newly formed song in their heart. It is sweet and silly all at once when they sing a made-up song to us. And then comes the familiar request: "Now you, Daddy! Now you!" So, when my girls were young, I would make up silly songs about them. The songs contained the details of the moment—how pretty they are, their sweet personalities, or how funny they could be. But the real reasons that a grown man will make up a silly song for his daughters is clear—they are precious to me. No matter what they do, I see them as lovely, but that's not why they are loved. Our children are intrinsically valuable to us simply because they are our children.

I fear the church rejoices over things different than what causes God to rejoice. We have trained ourselves to rejoice, using the same measures Wall Street uses: number of clients and level of income. Too often, we rejoice over the number of programs a church has implemented. The common theme of joy within our congregations is that of successful, powerful, productive ministry.

During Christ's ministry, He sent out 70 followers in teams of 2 so they could minister and proclaim the Messiah had come. As they returned, their reports were amazing—they even cast out evil spirits. "Can you believe this?" must have been a recurring phrase. Jesus helps them to refocus on the only source of true joy. *"However, don't rejoice that the spirits submit to you, but rejoice that your names are written in heaven"* (Luke 10:20). Forget about exercising spiritual power or having a total wipeout today. Do not overstate the success of what you saw occur and do not emphasize any failure you encountered. Rejoice in what causes the Father to rejoice.

Don't let the excitement over a large ministry, helping to build a big church, establishing a children's program, launching a great small group, or working on a missions project become the only priority in life. Don't boast that your ministry is small and therefore more intimate. Be excited over the greatest of all miracles—you have been redeemed and are rightly related to God! After all, that is what excites Him about you.

We should rejoice in the salvation of the lost and a repentant attitude among the saved. Luke 15 is the parable of things lost and found. In verse 6, the finder of lost things calls for neighbors to come over and do one thing: *"Rejoice with me, because I have found my lost sheep."* As the chapter continues, other finders issue the same call for celebration.

Please take a few moments for a simple exercise: Rejoice over your own salvation and in the salvation of others.

Restoring Love

Though we have been redeemed, we are not perfected yet. We stray. The Old Testament story of Hosea and Gomer is a provocative reminder of that fact. Hosea is commanded by God to take Gomer—a prostitute—as his wife. It is a living picture of God's restoring love for Israel.

Gomer's commitment, however, is short-lived. Even after having children with Hosea, she goes back to the streets to sell herself to the highest bidder. What is God's command to Hosea? Go and buy back your whorish wife from the marketplace. It is perhaps the most costly and embarrassing moment of his life. But it is also the most godly act he may ever commit.

Philip has said, "No other mortal man, in my opinion, has known the love of God more clearly than Hosea. It is a rare and high honor to serve as prophet to the Most High, but God asked Hosea to *live out* the message in the most personal of ways: a wedding, the marriage bed, and parenting. He *lives* the lesson that the Lord God is willing to pay the whole price it takes to keep us in right standing with Him."

After all, we sell ourselves so cheaply to the world. It is a pittance in comparison to the treasure of a relationship with the Father. Allegiance to the latest media technology, attention to a ball game, emotional energy over furnishing our home, detailed thinking about a project at work. It all seems so useless. C. S. Lewis said: "Indeed, if we consider the unblushing promises of reward and the staggering nature of the rewards promised in the Gospels, it would seem that Our Lord finds our desires not too strong, but too weak. We are half-hearted creatures, fooling about with drink and sex and ambition when infinite joy is offered us, like an ignorant child who wants to go on making mud pies in a slum because he cannot imagine what is meant by the offer of a holiday at the sea. We are far too easily pleased."[2] We lose track of the price that the second member of the Trinity has paid on our behalf. He has died so we might know God.

At the end of the Bible, we have the book of The Revelation. It is the apocalyptic view of the end of human history on Earth as we know it. Even in the one prophetic book of the New Testament, we get a view of God as He is still working to help the church live out the gift of redemption. In the first few chapters, the writer John pens seven letters to local churches, and we are hard-pressed to not avoid the vile church at Laodicea—it was lukewarm and nauseating to God. Yet in His letter to this church is the oft-quoted verse: *"Listen! I stand at the door and knock. If anyone hears My voice and opens the door, I will come in to him and have dinner with him, and he with Me"* (Revelation 3:20). Even to the wicked church, God stands at the door and awaits our repentance. If we humble ourselves, we can dine with Him again. As soon as we open the door, there is restoration—and it is time to celebrate!

The motif of the verse in Revelation causes us to flip back a few pages to the Epistle of James, who reminds the believers, *"Brothers, do not complain about one another, so that you will not be judged. Look, the judge stands at the door!"* (James 5:9). We must not miss the connection: Time is short, and He is standing at the proverbial door. The Lord is coming to judge or restore. Since God offers restoration to the wayward believer, we should be advocates for one another. We should be quick to personally enter back into the relationship with God and assist others in doing the same.

We do not do this out of pity for the wayward soul. We do it because we remember what it is like to have to return ourselves, broken and embarrassed at our failures. We do it because God accomplished restoration in us.

At the Father's direction, the Son was anointed and sent for a work that could not be accomplished by anyone else. Outside of Him, we are so impoverished of spirit we could not ever find our way to Him.

The heart of the Father ought to trump all of our pursuits—work, relationships, hobbies. • When I am about to lash out at my rogue child, what would be the heart of the Father?

• When I am ready to give up on an unbeliever, where is the Father?

• When I am at the end of a project, to whom do I give the credit?

• When I look at my spouse with love, what is the heart of the Father for him or her? Living in an intimate relationship with the Father and living according to His heart for others will solve a plethora of problems in ministry, family, and work. Submit to the heart of the Father.

Allow the Father to teach you of His heart for you, your family, your neighborhood, your culture. The missional outworking of His heart in our lives refuses to allow us to sit still. He drives us out into the rocky places of people's lives. Allying yourself with the Father's work is to travel with Him as He seeks those who are wayward.

Points for Personal Reflection and Group Discussion

1. How does being a parent change a person's life? What adjustments are made in your priorities?

2. How does parenting help you to better understand God's love?

3. Consider the nature of God's pursuing love in your own story of placing your faith in Jesus.

4. How can you (and your church, Bible study group, missions group, women's or men's group, etc.) begin pursuing unbelievers in your community more effectively? What are the needs present that you could meet as a bridge to conversations about God's love?

5. Read Exodus 34:14 again. Describe the comfort that comes from knowing God has a jealous love for you.

6. In what ways can church members imitate God's jealous love for the church to be presented in purity to Christ?

7. List ways for your church or group to begin celebrating people's faith in Christ in a more obvious manner.

8. Read the first three chapters of Hosea. Reflect on the lengths to which God has gone to redeem us.

Chapter 3

DYING LOVE

LOVE IN THE LIFE OF CHRIST

My grandparents were fascinating. They were Irish. My grandfather was even more Irish than the rest of us. He passed that Irishness on to his children and, to a lesser degree, his grandchildren.

Like many Irishmen I know, he didn't talk much about love. In fact, I can't think of a single time he told me he loved me, though I know he did. *Love* just wasn't a word used in our house very often. But he showed he loved me—time and time again—by challenging me to be the best I could be, sacrificing for me in ways I would not know until years later, and taking care of his family in a way he considered honorable. We were Irish, we were New Yorkers, and we showed love in the ways we knew.

My grandfather was a working-class man. As a young man after World War II, he began in the fire department. Eventually, he became a battalion chief in the New York City Fire Department. In his last post, his battalion had responsibility for a group of houses in southern Manhattan.

My mother once said to me, "Your grandfather was very brave." She was right. My grandfather told me stories about going into buildings consumed by fire. Burn marks on his body proved he was telling the truth. Once he told me why firefighters are heroes: It is not because of their bravery, but because "when everyone else runs away from danger, we run toward it." And so, whether it is a fire or some other sort of catastrophe, when others run away, heroes run toward. That's what makes them heroes.

Dying Love

The words *dying* and *love* don't seem to go together, yet at times, great sacrifice is involved with love. In fact, when called upon, some people die in the act of showing love. Love isn't simply daisies, poetry, and the pretty things of life. The most dramatic examples of love often involve death. Love is more than mere emotion; it involves great sacrifice. When we look at the life of Jesus, we get the picture of His dying love—and how it changes us.

We see this kind of love expressed in what some consider one of the clearest expressions of the gospel. Paul wrote in 1 Corinthians 15:1–4,

Now brothers, I want to clarify for you the gospel I proclaimed to you; you received it and have taken your stand on it. You are also saved by it, if you hold to the message I proclaimed to you —unless you believed for no purpose. For I passed on to you as most important what I also received: that Christ died for our sins according to the Scriptures, that He was buried, that He was raised on the third day according to the Scriptures.

These four verses are some of the most important in the Bible because they tell us what is most important—the Cross. We don't go to church to be good people, do nice things, or stay out of trouble. The Christian faith is not there simply to help us overcome certain emotional dysfunctions, solve relationship woes, and handle career crises—though that may be a result. The Bible reminds us of what is most important: the gospel expressed in the Cross.

The story of the modern-day martyr Jim Elliot is known by many. Jim and four other missionaries were killed by the very Ecuadorian tribesmen they hoped to reach with the gospel. As inspiring as their willingness to go to the ends of the earth, it is the story of Jim's wife, Elisabeth, that convicts me more. Even in the face of her husband's death, she still sought the redemption of the tribesman that killed her husband. Elisabeth—along with her young daughter—left the comforts of American culture to live in a foreign land to be on mission to those who hurt her deeply.

What is the gospel?

To understand the dying love of Christ, we've got to start with the gospel. Paul wrote, *"Now brothers, I want to clarify for you the gospel I proclaimed to you; you received it and have taken your stand on it. You are also saved by it, if you hold to the message I proclaimed to you —unless you believed for no purpose"* (1 Corinthians 15:1–2). This bold statement left the Corinthian church no choice but to listen intently and learn the gospel completely. The same must be true for us in our day.

I love church planters because they are so focused on reaching the lost and starting churches. At a church planting conference, I asked the audience of about 550 to pair up and answer three questions about one another.

First, I asked them to tell the person next to them what their new churches were doing to be culturally relevant. Immediately, everyone did so. And in 30 seconds they switched and let the other person answer the question. A distinct roar of enthusiasm filled the room.

Second, I asked them to tell one another what their churches were doing to engage their communities. Once again, they immediately turned to one another and talked passionately about engaging their communities. The roar gained momentum as each took a turn.

Then I asked, "What is the gospel?"

An eerie silence fell across the room. If ever there was a moment when missional church leaders would answer with a roar, I thought it would have been then. I'm glad they are seeking cultural relevance. I'm proud they are out in their communities. But I wish they would have defined the gospel with the same passion they had answered the other questions.

When we assume the gospel, we assume too much.

Summed up in one word, the gospel is Jesus. Jesus Christ is who He claimed to be. The Crucifixion/Resurrection event is the most important in human history. Here is how I define the gospel: *The gospel is the good news that God, who is more holy than we can imagine, looked upon with compassion, people who are more sinful than we would possibly admit, and sent Jesus into history to establish His Kingdom and reconcile people and the world to himself. Jesus, whose love is more extravagant than we can measure, came to sacrificially die for us so that, by His death and resurrection, we might gain through His death and resurrection and by his grace what the Bible defines as new and eternal life.*

What is most important?

Perhaps *important* is an overused word. It is *important* to eat breakfast and *important* to make it to school on time. It is *important* to do your best for the sake of the team and *important* to get a plate of brownies to the neighbor for watching the dog. It is *important* to read my Bible and *important* to get home in time for my favorite TV show.

Why is the gospel more important? Because of its content. While we place value on things only because of an emotional tie or the fact that it delivers a momentary break from the "busyness of life," the gospel stands above the routines of life. First Corinthians 15:3 gives us our boundary markers for it all: *"For I passed on to you as most important what I also received: that Christ died for our sins according to the Scriptures."*

The gospel is not an attitude of trying harder or the will to accomplish more religious work on behalf of God. It is not even a willingness to be a great minister or missionary. If we are simply trying to be better persons, no matter the motivation, then we've misunderstood the fundamental nature of the gospel. The gospel is what is of *first* importance: believing and receiving *"that Christ died for our sins according to the Scriptures."* Once we understand the gospel, then the change of life will follow. However, it is a devastating mistake if we get the cause (gospel) and effect (changed life) out of order.

And this is where the love of Christ comes in: *"But God proves His own love for us in that while we were still sinners, Christ died for us! Much more then, since we have now been declared righteous by His blood, we will be saved through Him from wrath"* (Romans 5:8–9).

We can never *show* the love of Christ until we *understand* the love of Christ. And we can never understand the love of Christ until we understand His death. And we can never understand the death of Christ until we understand why He died. And we can never understand why He died until we understand His holiness and our sin.

We are God's enemies because we choose to live in opposition to Him. We choose to live our own ways and, as a result, we go to war against God in our hearts. But He has a plan. God displayed His love for us by dying for us when we were His enemies. To understand that plan, we have to go on a brief, but important, journey.

God shows His love and deals with our sin through justification. *Justification* is a theological term that relates to our salvation and has a wonderfully simple meaning. *Justified* means that, despite my crimes, God is willing to acquit me because of what Jesus did for me. We get off the hook because Jesus takes our place in judgment.

Everyone is outside of a relationship with God and placed under judgment. God's wrath is more horrible than the human mind can imagine—a total separation from any relationship with Him due to their sinful nature. On earth, we suffer without His personal presence but enjoy a common grace given to all human beings. In eternity, however, His absence will be felt in a place of never-ending pain, sorrow, and darkness—a place in which not even a wisp of His grace is present.

We all are under the judgment of God because, as long as we are outside the faith, we are His enemies. You and I are not God's friends until He affects our relationship with Christ. *"For if, while we were enemies, we were reconciled to God through the death of His Son, then how much more, having been reconciled, will we be saved by His life!"* (Romans 5:10).

So what is *"most important"*? It is that God demonstrated His love for us through the Cross. We have turned love into an indefinable emotion, a quiver in our liver, a sweet feeling of enjoying someone's company. It is so much more. How did Christ demonstrate love? By dying.

Death is a relatively simple concept. Thought ceases. The heart stops. The body halts. Why would anyone allow this condition to be forced upon them? We would die for our children. We would die for our spouses. I hope I would die for my faith. But that's about where it ends.

Christ dies for the rebellious. The one divine and perfect man dies for everyone who is mortal and broken. What could motivate such an act? Christ's death was born out of His love for the crown jewel of creation: us. Dispatched by the Father on a mission, Jesus arrived and died so we might live. *"We have redemption in Him through His blood, the forgiveness of our trespasses, according to the riches of His grace that He lavished on us with all wisdom and understanding"* (Ephesians 1:7–8).

We are saved by the wealth of unmerited favor lavished on us, but it begins with blood. Blood spilled on a hillside of death. The Son of God suffers under divine wrath so you and I can receive eternal redemption.

What is redemption? Only coupon clippers use the word *redeem* anymore. Every time we visit the grocery store, the clerk asks, "Do you have any coupons to redeem?" *Redeem* means we are making a purchase with a substitute. At the store, the manufacturer authorizes that a piece of paper clipped from Sunday coupons is just as good as currency. In effect, they give up on some of what the consumer owes them in purchasing their product. The scraps from the newspaper are used in lieu of that which has real value. It's a way to buy something without personal cost. The payment needed to escape God's judgment was made on our behalf. Scraps cut from newspaper flyers might get us half price for a can of soup, but Christ paid the full price for our souls. That was Jesus' mission.

Think again about the heroic firefighter who runs into buildings while others are running out. Firefighters risk injury and death because they value the lives of families in their community. Jesus values us even more. He didn't die just to prove we were worth saving. His death was for our full redemption. By His blood, we are made fit to enter a personal relationship with the One who is *"the High and Exalted One"* (Isaiah 57:15).

As missional Christians, we must decide what will be most important and receive our undivided attention. Christ dying in love combines the power of life and death. It was not then—and is not now—politically correct or culturally expedient to express love through death. Yet that is the example we have in the Son of God.

What is the end result?

"That he was buried, that he was raised on the third day according to the Scriptures"

—1 CORINTHIANS 15:4

What is the point of dying love? It doesn't make sense for someone to love you deeply and then intentionally leave you to die. However, 1 Corinthians 15:4

gives us the truth of the story, the gospel in miniature. It goes beyond Jesus' death to His resurrection.

Jesus' resurrection opens the way for us to a new life. As the death of Christ was a sacrifice of love, so the resurrection of Christ was His victory in love. Remember what 1 John 4:19 says: *"We love because he first loved us."* As Christians, we should be the most loving people in the world.

Planting a church will drive this point home. Through leading church plants, we have encountered many people who were willing to discover the gospel with us, simply because we loved them. They were fully aware we disagreed with them about beliefs. But because we worked at being a people marked by love, they were willing to come into our worship services, attend our home Bible study groups, and serve the community with us while they discovered the gospel of Christ.

Unfortunately, that isn't everyone's experience. Many people are losing faith in the church. They don't see the church as a place of love but of judgment. Perhaps it's not because the lost misperceive us but because we don't love them enough. A Gallup poll spoke to the issue of trust among Americans: "Americans trust the military and the police force significantly more than the church and organized religion. . . . Only 46 percent of respondents said they had either a 'great deal' or 'quite a lot' of confidence in the church, compared with 69 percent who said they trusted the military and 54 percent who trust police officers. The figures are among the lowest for institutionalized religion in the three and a half decades Gallup has conducted the poll. Peaking at 68 percent in May 1975, the numbers bottomed out at 45 percent in June of 2003."[1]

The Most Loving Act of Human History

We are people who have been bought—there's that "redeemed" idea again—by the most loving act of human history. Yet we have often failed to live up to the love it demonstrates.

"As the Father has loved Me, I have also loved you. Remain in My love. If you keep My commands you will remain in My love, just as I have kept My

Father's commands and remain in His love. I have spoken these things to
you so that My joy may be in you and your joy may be complete. This is My
command: Love one another as I have loved you. No one has greater love
than this, that someone would lay down his life for his friends."
—JOHN 15:9–13

The Son of God ties together the end result of love. In relation to everyone else, we are to live by the example of how Jesus has loved us. When Jesus said that we are to love each other in the same way He loved us (v. 12), we are given no room for equivocation. He presses the point and reminds us that the greatest expression of love is in giving up one's own life (v. 13). Because we have died to ourselves through being crucified with Christ, the way we love should be different from the world. The death of Christ upon the Cross makes it possible for missional believers to live lives of love.

Perhaps we could even say, if we aren't on Christ's mission of love, we are looking down at the work of the Cross, not fully understanding it. We are ignoring its implications. The endgame for us ought to be a life within us that is different because of the presence of the Savior who died and rose for us.

Will we be called upon to die? Physically—maybe not, even though many believers in our modern times still face death for their faith. Spiritually—most definitely. We must die to self. Our dreams, aspirations, and intentions outside of God's agenda must fall away. The desire for Christ's glory and gospel must be the foremost passion in us, in such a way that all other desires fade.

Are you willing to be a hero?

As my grandfather taught me, a hero is someone who goes into places and accomplishes things other people don't want to do or simply can't do. They are not the easiest things to do, and it takes more than most of us can handle.

I am always a bit amused when a flight attendant asks me if I am willing to be a hero. As a frequent flyer, I can often get the exit row, but it appears only heroes are allowed to sit in exit rows. Time after time, sitting in a plane, the flight attendant walks up and says, "You are sitting in an exit row. Are you willing to help in the event of an emergency?" My vocal response is a confident, "Yes." Yet I think, "If you mean help as in I'm going to open the door, jump out before everybody else, and get out of their way, then, yes, I am ready and willing to help."

But then the flight attendant presses the issue. "Well, you might have to stay and hold the door." My reply is not as confident: "Well, let's go with that for the moment, and we'll just see how things unfold."

The attendant looks at me like I'm crazy. Why? Because I'm not a hero. I'd probably stay and help, but who knows how I'd react in the heat of the moment. Some run into the devastation; that's heroism.

Many of us want to be a hero. As children, we dream of awaking with superpowers of strength, flight, telepathic powers, and invincibility. We don't lose this compulsion when we grow up, but our heroes change. We have the hope to be great leaders like King Leonidas of Sparta in the fifth century, who stood, though outnumbered. We want the internal strength of Rosa Parks, who simply sat down for justice in Montgomery. We even dream of defeating the bad guys like our favorite heroes from the latest action movie.

When we consider the heroes of human history (and imagination), we seldom think of Christ, yet look at His life. When everyone else was running away, He runs straight into the most important event in human history—the Cross. And in running to the Cross, He does more than die. Dying is as heroic an action as one can take, but Jesus' death is more than an example. He became sin on our behalf. His death overcomes the power of sin. This is the ultimate love—and the ultimate death. This is the ultimate heroism lived out.

So, would you sacrifice yourself for someone or something? We have all asked ourselves that question. The beauty of the Scriptures' teaching is that because of the Cross, we will not have to die for the others. Jesus already died for us. We simply live differently because of His death. As believers, our lives will be marked by a love powered by a cross and an empty tomb.

So in light of the Cross, how then will you live?

• Lead a church known for its love of one another and the city.

• Be a parent who pours out herself for the children she loves but are sometimes ungrateful.

• Lead your family toward the adventure of the gospel-centered life.

One day Plutarch the philosopher was looking attentively at a pile of bones when Alexander the Great walked by him. He asked Plutarch what he was looking for. The philosopher answered, "That which I cannot find: the difference between your father's bones and the bones of his slaves." At the end of our lives, there will be nothing significant or unique in what remains of us physically. Our mark on the world will be left in what we deposited in the lives of others. Today, answer the question for yourself: Will my life be marked by the love that comes because of what Christ has done on the Cross?

We are all trying to learn to love like Christ. Learning is an odd endeavor. We learn to work by working, to speak by speaking, to study by studying, and to run by running. But love is different. We learn to love by dying.

Being Heroes

In the early 1980s, I was a big fan of Christian music. One of the songs that affected me greatly was Steve Taylor's "Hero."

> When the house fell asleep there was always a
> > light
> and it fell from the page to the eyes of an American
> > boy
> in a storybook land I could dream what I read when
> it went to my head I'd see
> I wanna be a hero
>
> Chorus:
> Hero
> it's a nice-boy notion that the real world's gonna
> > destroy
> you know
>
> it's a Marvel comic book Saturday matinee fairytale,
> > boy

Growing older you'll find that illusions are brought
and the idol you thought you'd be was just another
  zero
I wanna be a hero

Heroes died when the squealers bought 'em off
died when the dealers got 'em off
welcome to the "in it for the money as an idol"
  show
when they ain't as big as life
when they ditch their second wife
where's the boy to go?
gotta be a hero

(Chorus)

When the house fell asleep
from a book I was led to a light that I never knew
I wanna be your hero
and he spoke to my heart from the moment I
  prayed
here's a pattern I made for you
I wanna be your hero

"Hero"
written by Steve Taylor

From childhood to adulthood, we are hoping to be someone's hero. The scene we hope for is that of our children saying, "Thanks—now I know how to live and die for my children." It is as if we can pass into eternity because we leave behind a legacy where love is the centerpiece.

Jesus not only died to redeem us, but He also made a pattern for us to follow. He calls us—He compels us to love.

Points for Personal Reflection and Group Discussion

1. What is the gospel? Discuss the answer to this question that quieted a room of passionate church planters. Why is it important to be able to explain what the gospel is?

2. How can understanding the ideas of gospel, justification, and redemption help us understand dying love? What will it take to passionately love Christ and what could result?

3. Christ's dying love went beyond dying all the way to the Resurrection. Why is the Resurrection important to us?

4. Some Christians are enthusiastic when it comes to talking about the gospel, while others are more hesitant. What would it take to raise our level of passion for sharing the gospel with others?

5. Discuss the person you know who, when you think of them, the first thing that comes to mind is how well they love others. What about your faith in Christ can help you to live out this important part of our new life in Him?

6. Jesus not only redeemed us—but He made a pattern for us to follow. What are some illustrations from His life of how He loved others, and how can we follow them more closely?

7. First Corinthians 15:1–4 speaks of the importance of the Cross. How do you understand the connection between love and dying? What is in your life to which you should die in order to love better?

Chapter 4

INDWELLING LOVE

THE SPIRIT'S LIVING LOVE

S onny is a piece of work. He showed up about six months after the start of our church plant. He was on our prospect list from a phone campaign, and I talked to him a few times on the phone. Then he showed up. And to say that he was a challenge would be quite the understatement.

He began attending reluctantly. Initially, Philip built a friendship with him and Sonny kept coming, but not really knowing why. Sonny felt compelled to attend worship services and seek the truth. From the outset, it was obvious the Spirit was drawing him to salvation.

He was a Vietnam War vet who served in the armed forces—and also behind bars. A construction foreman by trade, he lived a hard life and it showed. Sonny's journey was both troubled and amazing. And every Sunday morning, Sonny showed up early with donuts and chocolate milk for the kids in our church.

Although Philip invested the most in Sonny, everyone shared with him how to follow Christ. But his journey stalled. His attitude vacillated between worse and improved. We were the external witnesses of the internal conviction of God's Spirit in his life.

A weekend car accident seemed to bring Sonny's spiritual quest to a crashing halt. After being hit in traffic, Sonny lost his temper with the other driver and then with the police. He wasn't very good at keeping quiet, and eventually the officers put him in handcuffs to control him. As a result of "sharing his views" with the judge, the judge handed Sonny a 30-day jail sentence.

When Sonny arrived at church the day after his sentencing, he blamed everyone else but himself for what happened. Then he explained he would return to jail within a few days. As his pastors, we knew it was time for him to face his own character issues and see his need for the Spirit's permanent presence in his life.

In the back of the high school auditorium where we met, I told Sonny that God was using his circumstances to draw him to Himself. Sonny abruptly and graphically told me what I could do with my opinion, and we grieved as he walked away from the high school that morning without even attending the service. Although we didn't see it at the time, God's Spirit wasn't finished with him.

Sonny left for home, but in his anger he made a couple of wrong turns.

Each one increased his anger. Enraged, he yelled at God and asked why He was such a harsh God. Then he saw a sign for a storefront church he'd seen before but never taken notice of. Still very angry with God, he wheeled his truck into a parking space. Seeing his anger, the people on the sidewalk moved out of his way as he stormed through the front door of the church. Murmuring like a Hebrew in the desert, he sat in the back row of another church. But before the service was over, he knew God had brought him to the right place.

We had lost contact with Sonny. He didn't answer his phone and would not return any of our messages. We feared for him and prayed fervently to see him change. Then, nearly six months later, Sonny called Philip. Sonny asked if Philip and his family would attend his baptism service. Whoa! What had happened? He went on to explain what we had always said—"The Spirit is working in you and one day you are going to surrender your life to Christ"—had come true. He was committing himself to following Jesus by placing his faith in Him and was ready to publicly confess his new faith through baptism.

Although it was hard for us to let him go, our part of Sonny's journey was over. The Spirit had been working on him before we ever met him, and He'll continue to mold him to look like Christ long after he's forgotten us. Our friendship with Sonny is a living reminder that God the Spirit works in and through us because of His great fondness for redeeming people.

The Holy Spirit at Work

First Corinthians 2:1–16 tells us how the Holy Spirit works. Sonny's story may be much like your own or that of someone you know. A person may come close, maybe even desiring to understand God, but resist the probing of God's Spirit. Anger, denial, and self-justification can reign supreme, but those attitudes are no match for the Spirit of God when He begins His work within us. We can only resist Him until we come to the "aha!" moment that changes everything.

Sonny came to that place, and suddenly he saw what God had prepared for him and had so freely given to him. God revealed it by His Spirit. In that moment, Sonny knew he'd started a journey initiated by the Spirit of God, and he wanted to share it with Philip and his new church family. We can allow anger, denial, and self-justification to rule our lives, but those attitudes are no match for the Spirit of God when He begins His work within us.

We are familiar with the heart of the Father and the work of the Son. However, too many are puzzled with the Holy Spirit. We know He's here, but we can't see Him. His work becomes blatantly evident when we look for it, but we are a bit uncertain about what to do with Him.

The Counselor must come

Many of us wish Jesus would just come down from heaven and sit with us for a few moments. It seems like it would be so much simpler to have Him in person. But what did Jesus say about such an attitude? He told His closest followers, *"Nevertheless, I am telling you the truth. It is for your benefit that I go away, because if I don't go away the Counselor will not come to you. If I go, I will send Him to you"* (John 16:7).

Having Jesus with us physically right now, full-time, sounds like a great idea. But in John 14 and 16, He explains why it is so important that the Counselor comes in His place. God's eternal desire is to have a personal relationship with us. Though sin separates us from God, He seeks us out. Though we are marred by iniquity, He died for us. Though we are weak, as we will see in studying the role of the Spirit, He desires to aid us in faithful, missional living.

Once we enter into a *saving relationship* with the Lord through repentance and faith in Him, we are no longer the same; we have the presence of God the Spirit dwelling inside of us. This presence is love, and we did not come to it on our own. This indwelling is God's gift, and His presence is now within us. The addition of God's presence in our lives is in fact the presence of true love. It is through His love that He works within us to make us more loving like God. Then, the Holy Spirit compels us toward the mission of God.

He empowers the message

When I came to you, brothers, announcing the testimony of God to you, I did not come with brilliance of speech or wisdom. For I didn't think it was a good idea to know anything among you except Jesus

Christ and Him crucified. I came to you in weakness, in fear, and in much trembling. My speech and my proclamation were not with persuasive words of wisdom but with a powerful demonstration by the Spirit, so that your faith might not be based on men's wisdom but on God's power.

—1 CORINTHIANS 2:1–5

The gospel is the most important message in human history because it communicates the character and work of God. It brings hope, salvation, and peace. Philip attended a retreat with a few other church planters some time ago. One night, as they returned to the hotel after dinner, a guy approached them, hoping to find a party. He had a wealthy family, motorcycles, and a girlfriend who was a dancer. He had what men of the world want: exciting travel, expensive toys, and a beautiful woman other men desire. Interestingly, the fellow stayed to talk, even after finding out what the church planters "did for a living." He finally asked, "What do you have that I don't?" The answer was easy: *hope.* He didn't want their vocation, but he did want what characterized their lives. The group knew the Holy Spirit's presence made the difference. It made their lives curious to him, even enviable.

The Corinthians were a metropolitan people of business, arts, wealth, culture, music, and religion. Corinth was *the* place to live, but it also was a place of great depravity; every desire of the flesh could easily be gratified. Paul came to them, knowing the gospel presentation had to go beyond mere human trappings or charisma. In fact, he resolved to know nothing *"except Jesus Christ and Him crucified."* God's presence empowers this most foolish message.

Even Paul had a comfort zone

When you and I step out of our comfort zones to share the message of eternal darkness and salvation, we experience some anxiety. Even Paul shared this emotional connection with us. On one level, this statement by the über-Apostle may shock us. We expect to hear Paul thunder away at the sinners and eloquently encourage the believers. This well-educated man of Jewish culture, transformed by Christ, who always presented the gospel with power, readily admits he often spoke *"in weakness, in fear, and with much trembling"* (1 Corinthians 2:3). Perhaps he understood the statement from Zechariah 4:6, *"'Not by strength or by might, but by My Spirit,' says the Lord of Hosts."*

We will often encounter people who are intelligent and have set their own defense against faith in Christ. However, we must still bear witness for Christ and the change He has affected in our lives. Oftentimes, we can get an irreligious person to conclude, "I need Jesus." But it is not my own intelligence or your charisma or that person's force of will that is required for sharing the gospel. It's an eternal message with eternal consequence; it's only by the work of the Spirit that a human soul is convinced.

The Holy Spirit expresses God's compassionate work of salvation through our witness. For there to be any effect, we must have the accompaniment of the Spirit with the gospel presentation. The evidence of His presence could be the drama of a miracle or a life changed by God's grace. Some of us experienced a radical turnaround as adults, while others were saved in childhood. Others experience severe inner turmoil of conviction before they are convinced of the gospel. But no one comes to saving knowledge of Christ apart from the presence of God's Spirit.

Paul writes, *"For even the Messiah did not please Himself. On the contrary, as it is written, The insults of those who insult You have fallen on Me"* (Romans 15:3). The empowering presence of the Spirit brings amazing hope. People without hope are everywhere, and our role is to glorify God by offering hope through the message of the gospel.

When He comes, He will convict the world about sin, righteousness, and judgment: About sin, because they do not believe in Me; about righteousness, because I am going to the Father and you will no longer see Me; and about judgment, because the ruler of this world has been judged.

—JOHN 16:8–11

The Spirit empowers us as we share the gospel and encourage believers. We must remember, His missional role is to convict; our missional role is simply to go.

Love is the place where *our going* and *His convicting* converge. Since the Holy Spirit could do His work without us, why would He choose to use such imperfect instruments? Because His desire for an intimate love relationship for us is so deep that He wants us to participate in His redeeming work. By the Spirit's presence, we can then be compelled by love to move out of our comfort zone and into the world where a hearing and demonstration of the gospel is needed.

He instructs the members

Unfortunately, as we see on TV and elsewhere, some people say the Holy Spirit instructed them to do some pretty bizarre things. Nevertheless, the Holy Spirit does speak and continues to speak to us. Scripture teaches what the Spirit actually does in our lives:

However, we do speak a wisdom among the mature, but not a wisdom of this age, or of the rulers of this age, who are coming to nothing. On the contrary, we speak God's hidden wisdom in a mystery, a wisdom God predestined before the ages for our glory. None of the rulers of this age knew this wisdom, for if they had known it, they would not have crucified the Lord of glory. But as it is written: What eye did not see and ear did not hear, and what never entered the human mind—God prepared this for those who love Him. Now God has revealed these things to us by the Spirit, for the Spirit searches everything, even the depths of God. For who among men knows the thoughts of a man except the spirit of the man that is in him? In the same way, no one knows the thoughts of God except the Spirit of God. Now we have not received the spirit of the world, but the Spirit who comes from God, so that we may understand what has been freely given to us by God.

We also speak these things, not in words taught by human wisdom,
but in those taught by the Spirit, explaining
spiritual things to spiritual people.

—1 CORINTHIANS 2:6–13

All our spiritual experiences should be filtered through Scripture to prove their validity. If left to our own devices, we will eventually seek what is pleasurable to the flesh and leave behind what is glorious to God. The Spirit reveals the deep truths of God. God is love, and expressions of love are central to His instruction.

Here, Paul says the wisdom of this world "are coming to nothing." The rulers of this world were so unaware of spiritual wisdom that they killed the Son of Glory; a most unloving act—killing the only truly innocent man. The Spirit seeks to orient people to the agenda of God. This is why Jesus said—*"I do not call you slaves anymore, because a slave doesn't know what his master is doing. I have called you friends, because I have made known to you everything I have heard from My Father"* (John 15:15). The desire of the Son is to show us what the Father is doing. Thus, the Spirit has come to indwell the believer so we will understand what the Son is doing.

Reveals the truth

But as it is written: What eye did not see and ear did not hear, and
what never entered the human mind—God prepared this for those
who love Him. Now God has revealed these things to us by the
Spirit, for the Spirit searches everything, even the depths of God.

—1 CORINTHIANS 2:9–10

Here Paul has quoted from Isaiah, the Old Testament prophet. In the original passage, Isaiah asked God to reveal His plans and empower the powerless. We can't see God's complete work, or hear it, or even imagine the things that are in God's heart and mind. God, however, reveals them to us by His Spirit.

The eternal truths of God are too great for us to discern on our own. We can't reach out to Him or climb up to Him, force His hand, or convince Him to tell us His plan for today or tomorrow. He graciously and lovingly shows us what He will be doing. It takes humility on our part to listen and follow.

It's like a parent who has something little Susie needs to hear, but her focus is on playing with dolls, throwing rocks, discovering frogs, and annoying siblings. She can't seem to settle herself long enough to hear the good news that you want to take her to the ice cream shop. God shows us His heart for the mission of the church as we sit silently before the Spirit and the Scriptures.

The same is true of us as believers individually and as churches. The Spirit wants to teach us the deep truths of the Scriptures and lead us into the vast mission of God. We, in turn, must be more concerned with the compulsion of love than with the construction of ministry models. Love for God and the people He loves should drive us to learn the truths we are led to by the Spirit as He unfolds the beauty of the Bible to us.

Searches the truth

Now God has revealed these things to us by the Spirit, for the Spirit searches everything, even the depths of God. For who among men knows the thoughts of a man except the spirit of the man that is in him? In the same way, no one knows the thoughts of God except the Spirit of God. Now we have not received the spirit of the world, but the Spirit who comes from God, so that we may understand what has been freely given to us by God.

—1 CORINTHIANS 2:10–12

Paul teaches that the Spirit is searching *"the depths of God."* Searching the thoughts of another person is difficult indeed. My wife and I have been married for over 20 years, and I still don't always know what she is thinking! Out of love, we *want* to understand our spouse's thinking process, but it takes a lifetime to understand the nuances and complexities of another soul. Even then, I will fall short because I can't be inside her mind and heart. And what prospect do we have of completely understanding another when much of the time we don't even understand ourselves?

The only hope of understanding comes from the indwelling Spirit. God freely offers the gift of the Holy Spirit, who plumbs the depths of who He is *so* we can understand what is freely given to us. That which is freely given by God is most certainly not earned. The Spirit's presence brings about a greater depth of understanding of our salvation. Without His presence, believers would wallow in a sea of misunderstanding regarding our salvation. Through the Spirit's searching and His residence within us, we can properly relate to our salvation, which guards us from excessive liberty-taking and harsh legalism.

But be warned: It's foolish to think we have come to a full understanding of our salvation. Apart from Him, we can't know what He is doing in the kingdom; we can't understand the full measure of what Christ endured or what the Spirit is doing day by day. Yet that is the role of the Spirit—to give us understanding of the deep things God is accomplishing in our lives.

The Spirit, because He is God, is able to search for the truth needed in our lives. From the mundane activity of daily chores to the sublime engagement in our mission of reconciliation, He is able to deliver to us the truth we need for the assignment He has given.

Therefore, we should not squander the gift of the Spirit's presence in our lives. It's time to go beyond the five-minute morning devotional that is merely a quick-witted spur for the day's activities. Rather, the insight from God's presence should be valued enough that we give Him opportunity to reveal His thoughts to us. Our devotions should be intentionally focused on the truth of God's love, received through the presence of the Spirit.

Teaches the truth

I see a missional movement in Paul's words. *"We also speak these things, not in words taught by human wisdom, but in those taught by the Spirit, explaining spiritual things to spiritual people"* (1 Corinthians 2:13). What we learn by the Spirit, we are to express in spiritual means. We do not put it on display behind glass. Rather, the Spirit's wisdom is to be taken out of the collector's case and put into action. Perhaps the greatest tragedy that occurs in churches is when the deep treasures of God, which once were taught, are no longer spoken about in the company of faith. We keep these truths to ourselves and no longer reveal them. It is the supreme tragedy because we are withholding from others God's offer of intimacy.

Protected or engaged?

Philip attended a Christian university. Most of the student body poked fun at the school by nicknaming it "the Bubble." It was a safer environment than the real world. They were protected but not often engaged into the compelling ministry of the Spirit. The students learned, unfortunately, to compartmentalize spirituality and speak of it only in religion courses. Expectations meant they were to be Christians but not to fully live out their faith in every aspect of daily life in the world.

The Spirit's instruction, however, is intended to be applied, and the Spirit's application of truth has much to do with our gospel witness. We are called to make a choice between developing a Christian subculture and living as a counter-culture to the world. If we choose to hide, then all we've done is created an Amish version of evangelicalism. I don't think that is at all what God intended. We are to live in the world, but not like the world. We are to be a counter-culture, shaped by the Spirit, demonstrating lives changed by the gospel, and discussing it freely.

What are the normal subjects of our conversation? What do we find ourselves speaking about most often? It's fine to discuss family, hobbies, and the like. However, when we fall into a rut where we find it awkward to talk about what the Spirit is teaching us, we should evaluate whether we are allowing Him to dominate our lives. Since His love is great enough to indwell our feeble lives, we should respond to this love by applying the truth He reveals.

Communicating God's truth should be natural for missional believers. His words are so overwhelming that we cannot help but talk about such wondrous messages of hope and joy. But it must be done with respect for the truth (keeping it intact) and for the hearers (keeping them engaged).

I have found that people want to hear about these things. Perhaps in years gone by, a generational callousness developed to such conversation. But now our culture is sensitive to issues of spirituality. For example, when Philip was planting a church, some of his neighbors were nervous about interacting with him. There was an underlying fear of a one-way conversation with the preacher who thundered about the depth of their sinfulness, his words punctuated by the vigorous waving of a large King James Bible. He needed a different approach; he needed to listen to the Spirit and listen to his neighbors. In other words, love the Spirit enough to listen to Him and trust He is already working in his neighbors' lives—and love his neighbors enough to be sensitive to their needs. Now engaging with neighbors in a prepared manner is possible as the Spirit teaches him the deep things of God.

In the moment of conversation when people share portions of their spiritual journey, missional believers can remain in a state of astonishment at how the Spirit has prepared them weeks in advance for each conversation. He readies our minds and hearts to speak spiritual truths with spiritual words to those He has already been preparing. This stands as a living example of: *"But the Counselor, the Holy Spirit —the Father will send Him in My name —will teach you all things and remind you of everything I have told you"* (John 14:26).

He enables the mind

The Spirit of God has given us the mind of Christ (1 Corinthians 2:14–16), further described in Philippians 2:5–11. To summarize that passage, the mind of Christ is one of a humble slave. Just as Christ came as a servant to the Father, bringing salvation, we must seek how the Spirit would enable us to spiritually serve our neighbors today. How might we help them understand the gospel? After all, they can't understand it without the Spirit's help. As we are indwelt by the Spirit, we have the responsibility of sharing the gospel with them by using the spiritual truth God teaches us. He has enabled *our* mind, not theirs. This presents us with a missional duty to help our friends.

There are times when we speak to people about the things of God and they simply don't "get it." Guess what? They aren't supposed to understand, because they don't have the Spirit of God dwelling within them to interpret His truth. But as the Spirit draws them to be regenerated, they can come to believe and understand God's truth in their lives.

His presence changes us

As a believer, how is the presence of the Holy Spirit changing you in traffic jams, business meetings, at home, and elsewhere? God's presence in our lives makes an impact. Either we live joyful lives working with the Spirit, or we suffer constant conviction due to a rebellious heart.

Throughout the week, we may encounter those who are difficult to love. Perhaps now is the perfect time to search the Scriptures, allowing the Spirit to give us understanding of why God has placed that person in our life. Maybe God desires for us to show that person compassion and teach him or her the gospel. No doubt, we have a role to play in someone else's life.

In 2005, Hurricane Katrina ripped through the Gulf of Mexico and devastated the coastal cities. Most notably, New Orleans seemed like it was about to become a modern-day Atlantis, sinking into the sea. But help arrived, and the waters eventually receded. The amount of money and manpower spent on the Gulf Coast that year was astounding. The entire nation watched with pride as neighbors helped neighbors and people traveled from all over the country to aid in the recovery effort.

There was one unexpected effect, however: compassion fatigue for other needs. The agencies involved with helping families in the Southeast were flooded with donations and volunteers, but many other compassion organizations and benevolence funds suffered. There was only so much the population could give. By the time Christmas 2005 rolled around, many community food banks and shelters were in dire straits.

The American public had not been stingy. They had been exceedingly generous. Many had simply run out of resources to give, whether physically or financially. Their compassion resources had reached their limit.

Herein lies a great lesson concerning the role of the Spirit in our lives. He not only teaches us about love, He *is* love dwelling within us. As the recipient of

His indwelling presence, you are more than a student. You are a living conduit through which the Spirit extends the compassion and mercy of the Godhead to sinful and hurting people. He never tires of showing love. His judgment will come upon sin, but not due to a lack of love. His timing is perfect for all things, and we must simply allow His presence within us to work through us. Then, as missionaries to our community, we will never have a shortage of compassion for the church or the lost.

Points for Personal Reflection and Group Discussion

1. How have you viewed the Holy Spirit and His role in the past?

2. Looking back, share some of the ways that the Holy Spirit worked in your life to bring you to salvation in Christ. What are some specific ways He convicted you of sin and led you to a need of eternal hope?

3. The Spirit helps us to deal with troubling times, temptation, and learning new lessons. Which of these three has seemed most common in your life lately?

4. Describe a time when you shared a lesson from Scripture with a believing friend. How would you go about sharing one of those lessons with an unbeliever?

5. Read Philippians 2:5–11. What does it mean to have the same thinking (or mind) of Christ? What is the Holy Spirit teaching you that conforms your thinking to agree with Christ's mind?

6. To live the mission of God, we need the heart of God toward other people. How is the Holy Spirit helping to adjust your view of coworkers? Neighbors?

7. Review 1 Corinthians 2:13. What opportunities do you currently have to express spiritual truth with your friends and others whom Christ calls us to love?

Part II
Identifying Love:
the Church In the World

Chapter 5

IDENTIFIED BY LOVE

HAVING A MISSION THAT SHOWS

When my wife, Donna, and I discovered she was pregnant with our second daughter, we felt confident because we'd already been through it all with our first. That was before we worked out the route to the hospital.

We lived at one end of Georgia 400—with the hospital located at the other end of a constantly congested highway, jokingly referred to as the Atlanta Autobahn because it can take 45 minutes to travel 10 to 15 miles—on a good day.

When Donna's contractions started around 6:00 A.M. on a Friday morning, I explained to her that this was not a good day; morning rush hour was a bad time on any day to travel the Atlanta Autobahn. I casually mentioned we wouldn't want to join the Georgia 400 Club, named for babies born on the shoulder of the highway.

Just as I started to ask, "Can't this wait until later?" Donna's water broke, and we rushed out the door straight into . . . rain.

Now, I don't know why, but Georgians tend to randomly crash into each other on rainy days. (Maybe New Yorkers do it too, but I'm from there and just don't want to admit it.) That's exactly what they were doing as we drove as fast as we could—five miles an hour.

I called the hospital and they reassured me we were close. If we didn't make it in time, they said, we should remain calm, pull to the side of the road, and they'd talk me through the delivery. I looked at Donna for a moment. Then I said, "Hey, honey, they say we're going to make it!"

And I sped up to six miles an hour!

Whose bad day is this?

When we reached the hospital, the staff was waiting to rush Donna to the delivery room, where the nurses went to work. As they prepared Donna for the miracle of birth, the nurses stayed focused on each other, discussing details of their work and lives. One nurse seemed to be having a rough day. She spent about ten minutes complaining about her husband, job, and kids as Donna lay there in labor, trying to maintain some sweet charm. I said, "I know you must be having a bad day, but my wife is having a hard day too. She's having contractions. Would you mind taking this conversation outside?"

Both nurses started to get upset, but then stopped talking. One nurse quickly left, but the unhappy one remained.

"What do you do?" she asked.

"I'm a pastor."

"Really! I'm a Christian!" she responded. "What kind of pastor?"

I wanted to snap, "Not a very good one; now go away." Instead I named my denomination.

"Me too," she said.

Which leads to the point of this chapter: Why is it that many of the unhappy people we meet turn out to be church people? In fact, in my experience, some believers seem to think being unhappy and complaining is the mark of a mature Christian. It's as if grumbling has been added to the list of spiritual gifts. Sadly, this attitude increasingly seems to define churches. Instead, the connection of love in everyday life should identify the church as sent by Christ to make a difference.

Christians known by love

A study from LifeWay Research reflects my point: 58 percent of those studied stopped coming to church because of relational problems. For example, 26 percent said church members seemed judgmental or hypocritical; 20 percent didn't feel connected to people in the church; and 15 percent said churches were either unfriendly, unwelcoming, or cliquish.

Their experience in church seems quite the opposite from a song popular when I was young. Do you remember, "They'll Know We Are Christians"?

> We will work with each other, we will work side by side.
> And we'll guard each one's dignity and save each one's pride.
> And they'll know we are Christians by our love, by our love.
> They will know we are Christians by our love.
> By our love, by our love.

We will walk with each other, we will walk hand in hand.

And together we'll spread the news that God is in our land.

And they'll know we are Christians by our love, by our love.

They will know we are Christians by our love.

"They'll Know We Are Christians" by Peter Scholtes

Odd that "God is love"?

It seems natural that Christians should be known by their love, when you consider the Bible tells us *"God is love"* (1 John 4:16). Yet, the phrase *God is love* is a bit odd for the way we normally describe someone. We say Joan is athletic, Donna is beautiful, Bob is compulsive. We describe people by identifying a characteristic we see in them. And yet, when the Bible says, *"God is love,"* it means something different.

Scripture isn't saying He is a loving God (although He is). It isn't saying that when we think about love, we need to think about God. Neither is it saying God is *like* love. Rather, God actually *is* love. It is a trait, a characteristic that finds its origins in the nature of God. It is not earthly. It isn't human or common. It is a *divine* love.

Unfortunately, the church is known as many things today. Collectively, Christians are seen as one of several moral standards for the culture, as a political voting bloc, sometimes even as a hypocritical mass. Yet God didn't create the church to establish political, ethical, or sociological positions. Instead, the church is to be known as an extension of God's character: It should be known as the embodiment of love spoken and expressed.

One such illustration of the church in action might be surprising to some. When pastor Jerry Falwell passed away, he left a national legacy much different from the one he left through his local congregation. To a vast majority of people, Falwell was either a man to love or a man to loath. The popularized image of

Falwell was a caricature of his real life. In the popular press, he was a political figure who claimed God as a partisan.

However, those who knew him personally as a pastor and college president witnessed him found a home for unwed mothers and one for alcoholics in recovery. The amount of work he led for the poor, marginalized, and disenfranchised would amaze many. But most people—believers and nonbelievers—simply saw him as the head of the Moral Majority, seeking to dominate the Republican Party.

It's sad to have the summary of your time on earth be so mistaken. But, as the church, we should realize that we will often be portrayed incorrectly. So we must try all the more to love as God loves. When everything is said and done, we hope those who know us say we looked like our God— who is love.

A "tell-and-show" love

As a church, we're called to express *"God is love."* A helpful book, *Transformation: How Global Churches Transform Lives and the World,* by Bob Roberts, asks, "What if the church was a combination of Billy Graham and Mother Teresa?" This illustration is not meant to reflect correct theology, but it does give a quick "visual" of two approaches to teaching people about the good news from God. The point is: How would the church be different if we were known for *telling* people about Jesus and His love as well as *showing* people what Jesus did with His love? We need to embrace that the mission of the church is found both in the demonstration and proclamation of the gospel.

Therein is the challenge. The world sees the church as a minority with an agenda. What the world should see is the love of God expressed through faithful missional living. Our agenda as Jesus followers is not the sappy "be nice to everybody" sort of love. Mark Twain once reportedly remarked, "Church is where good people stand in front of good people and tell them how to be good people." That would be a sad agenda. We have the heroic agenda of love seen in Christ and the Cross and an empty tomb. So let's look at how we live out this love.

The early church showed the heroic love of Christ

When the church began, it emphasized devotion to God and concern for others. But somehow it lost its way and the church became known for everything but love. *Cities of God: The Real Story of How Christianity Became an Urban Movement and Conquered Rome*, by sociologist Rodney Stark, points out that first-century Christianity was not the worldwide phenomenon we often think it was. It was not even a major movement within the Roman Empire. Christians were in some of the major cities, but Christianity was still looked down upon by most of society.

The second century, however, brought two massive plagues that killed millions across the Roman Empire. Christianity exploded after the first plague and again after the second. Rodney Stark explains:

> Christian values of love and charity, from the beginning, had been translated into norms of social service and community solidarity. When disasters struck, the Christians were better able to cope, and this resulted in substantially higher rates of survival. This meant that in the aftermath of each epidemic, Christians made up a larger and larger percentage of the population even without new converts.[2]

Examining the historical records of the day, Stark also found that when the plagues hit, almost everyone abandoned the cities, fled into the hills, and sealed off the borders so no one could come in. Except for the Christians. They stayed and they cared for the sick and dying. Doesn't that remind you of the heroic love of Christ?

The church was still controversial. Christians still stood against the weak morals toward sexuality among the Romans (which is an ongoing issue in many cultures), against the greed of Roman life, and against emperor worship. But something happened when they became known for God's love. The favor of the people was won by this love.

Conventional thought, however, doesn't always reflect that perception. Many people think of the Crusades and blame the church: "Well, that wasn't an example of love." They are right. Grave sins have been committed in the name of "the church." But it is still obvious that love was central to faith and life in the early church. Acts 2:42–47 describes that love in the fellowship (eating together), toward God (praising God), and to the community (enjoying their favor). The passage ends: *"And every day the Lord added to them those who were being saved"* (v. 47). The church enjoyed a growing group of believers because they demonstrated love by living out the gospel.

Love must be central in our modern church as well. In order to see God adding to our number daily, the church must be marked by love; it has to be filled with loving people. Our mission is an evidence of God's love. Much of our challenge is wrapped up in the dual responsibility of *showing* love and *telling* truth. After all, telling the truth doesn't always breed popularity.

Showing love and telling truth today

During an interview, a reporter from a major newspaper asked me a pointed question. After talking generally about the changing face of religion in North America, the reporter asked if evangelicals would move away from the idea that homosexuality is wrong because the church is "all about love."

Because of God's Word and His nature, I answered honestly according to my convictions about both. I said something like: "Well, I know this probably doesn't sound very loving to you, but we think God has a perfect plan, and God laid out His plan eternally in His Word, the Bible. We think the most loving thing to do is tell the truth, even if that means disagreeing about someone's most personal choices for life."

The reporter surprised me when she said that seemed to make sense, but she still wanted to know if that view would harm people's view of the church. We all know the answer: In some cases it will, but how people *view* us is not the point. The truth *as given by God* is the point.

The most loving thing is not to go along with everyone's ideas and thoughts. Mankind's thoughts and ideas are destructive when they spring from earthly wisdom. Our kids don't get to do whatever they want, and God doesn't let us do whatever we want either. Why? Because He has a better plan. And so love marks our church. Now, that doesn't mean we aren't controversial for the stands we take on moral issues, but it should cause the world to notice a difference in the way we behave in the conflict.

We must find ways to live as a people marked by love:

We love because He first loved us. If anyone says, "I love God," yet hates his brother, he is a liar. For the person who does not love his brother he has seen cannot love the God he has not seen. And we have this command from Him: The one who loves God must also love his brother.

—1 JOHN 4:19–21

The source of love—intimacy with God—should drive humility into the very depths of our souls. You and I are not naturally inclined to be loving. But, as believers, we are to be responsive in our love toward God. Ultimately, love is not defined by the external affirmations of affection. Our love must be characterized by a responsiveness that not only loves God but also all those He places in our path. So the reason we show love is not because we want to, but because God first loved us. That's what marked the church and how the church lived—because God first loved her.

Scripture uses strong language about the love God bestows upon the church and Christians.

I was made a servant of this gospel by the gift of God's grace that was given to me by the working of His power. This grace was given to me —the least of all the saints—to proclaim to the Gentiles the incalculable riches of the Messiah, and to shed light for all about the administration of the mystery hidden for ages in God who created all things. This is so God's multi-faceted wisdom may now be made known through the church to the rulers and authorities in the heavens. This is according to His eternal purpose accomplished in

*the Messiah, Jesus our Lord. In Him we have boldness
and confident access through faith in Him.*

—EPHESIANS 3:7–12

This passage says the love of God is so strong for the church that He plans to use it as the instrument for revealing His wisdom to the world. At the time, it would have appeared to be a ludicrous statement, by human standards. To some, it still is.

A poem of love

These strange verses dropped into the middle of Ephesians tell us God has placed Jesus in charge of the church and that the church, ultimately, is going to change the world: *"And He put everything under His feet and appointed Him as head over everything for the church, which is His body, the fullness of the One who fills all things in every way"* (Ephesians 1:22–23). So we should take note of who the church is.

Don't miss the progression: As God is love . . . and has shown His love through Jesus . . . and has put Jesus in charge over the church . . . and given the church a mission . . . a call to love . . . and the mission is an expression of God's fullness in us . . . then the mission we have is compelled by love. That love is caring for the poor, our family, our neighbors. That love governs how we react and relate to one another. That love compels us to tell the truth, even when it isn't popular. It reminds us to share the love of God as expressed through the Cross of Christ.

All those things are proper and appropriate expressions of love as lived out through the life of God's church. It's not always the easiest thing to do, but these result from intimacy with God and the expression of His love to others.

We hear much about love from sources outside the church when the church itself should be the one speaking about love. One story is told about the Christian musician Michael W. Smith. The band U2's lead singer, Bono, asked Michael how to dismantle an atomic bomb. Michael didn't have an answer. Bono simply replied, "Love, with love."[3]

Now, not being a rocket scientist, I don't know the first thing about weapons of mass destruction, but the principle holds firm. Love is the key to transforming a lost world, ending all wars, ending all hunger, and healing all hurts. The generic feel-good, "I-love-everybody, hugs-all-around" kind of love will soothe a tired heart but will not last. The love of God expressed in Christ Jesus, however, changes the world.

God's love is sacrificial

As we discussed in a previous chapter, we should aspire to the level of God's sacrificial love. Ephesians 5:25–27—a passage focused on marriage—begins with *"Husbands, love your wives."* We could easily dive into the need for men to lead their families with love, but our study leads us to the other side of these verses. God chose marriage as a primary model of His love for His people. The Scriptures explicitly refer to the church as the Bride of Christ. Many people don't like churches. I get that. The church too often looks more like the ogre Shrek than the beautiful Bride. Sometimes the church is filled with people who, like me, are imperfect, who gossip, who are hypocrites. They are who I am and do what I do.

But you can't love Jesus and hate His Bride. You may become frustrated at a congregation, but you must love the church. He is her hero. And she is His beloved.

This symbolism is pressed to its limit. Christ, like any decent husband, is willing to give His life for the Bride. His ultimate aim is to make her holy. How did Christ love the church? He *"gave Himself for her, to make her holy, cleansing her in the washing of water by the word. He did this to present the church to Himself in splendor, without spot or wrinkle or anything like that, but holy and blameless"* (Ephesians 5:25–27).

Once again, the Cross comes crashing into the conversation. The necessary cleansing of the Bride comes through the action of Christ on the Cross. If you want to understand love, you've got to recognize that the central part of love is death. Only when we die can the mission of God take over—because then our desire for earthly gratification is suppressed.

Jesus didn't die on the Cross because the bad guys outwitted Him, or solely to be an example for us. He didn't die because He was looking for a spiritual act to accomplish (isn't that often how we decide whether to serve God and others?). Jesus died for the love held out to the church. In fact, His love began when there was conflict. *"But God proves His own love for us in that while we were still sinners, Christ died for us!"* (Romans 5:8). There is no way to view God as the big, vague bundle of love in the sky.

God showed love by choosing us

God's Word tells us the *why:*

> *For He chose us in Him, before the foundation of the world, to be holy and blameless in His sight.* **In love He** *predestined us to be adopted through Jesus Christ for Himself, according to His favor and will, to the praise of His glorious grace that He favored us with in the Beloved.*
>
> —EPHESIANS 1:4–6 (EMPHASIS ADDED)

Note the three beautiful words: *"In love He."* Because of His nature, God does an adopting work that surpasses all of humanity's compassion combined. Adoption is an amazing thing. A loving set of parents choose a child who has no merit above other children. There is no dowry that will reward the parents for their compassion; in fact, sometimes the opposite is true. Adoption is costly. It requires the parent to do all of the work, pay all of the price, and extend an immense amount of grace. The child can offer nothing but his or her presence in return. Adoption happens as the work of loving parents. In the same way, our spiritual adoption wasn't by chance or fortune, but in love. *"In love He"* is a phrase that should ring through the church every week as we consider the work of Christ on our behalf.

God's love as the standard for living

Seeing God's love for the church calls for a change in our lives. Instead of living out a sterile "From, Ed" in our relationships within the church, our lives become a living signature of love.

Why? Because God chose us and adopted us in love. He put us in the church for which He died, so He could make her holy and blameless (Ephesians 5:26). God has done all these things to demonstrate His love and bestow it on believers. This great love of God is demonstrated, not because of our favor in winning it, but because of who He is. It is His very nature.

There is one more passage of Scripture we should explore. It teaches us that "unloving Christian" is an oxymoron—a phrase where the words contradict one another, like "jumbo shrimp."

Dear friends, let us love one another, because love is from God, and everyone who loves has been born of God and knows God. The one who does not love does not know God, because God is love. God's love was revealed among us in this way: God sent His One and Only Son into the world so that we might live through Him. Love consists in this: not that we loved God, but that He loved us and sent His Son to be the propitiation for our sins. Dear friends, if God loved us in this way, we also must love one another. No one has ever seen God. If we love one another, God remains in us and His love is perfected in us.

—1 JOHN 4:7–12

Wow! There it is. Everything described in this chapter, summed up in one amazingly brief passage.

The great problem is, we know a lot of unloving Christians. Some of us could even point to unloving churches. We all would even have to admit that, at times, we have lived this oxymoronic life too. To that end, God works to change the passions and intentions of our hearts. He forms us to be like the Son. He knows that for the church to *tell* the gospel, it must *live* the gospel as well.

The life of the church must be a living, breathing expression of that love because it is founded in the One who *is* love, and He calls us to love.

The last words from Jesus recorded in Matthew's Gospel is commonly known as the Great Commission (28:18-20). In it, He teaches that we are responsible to "make disciples of all nations." (The next chapter will deal with it at length.) Earlier in the same book, we are given the Great Commandment in 22:37-40:

> *He said to him, "Love the Lord your God with all your heart, with all your soul, and with all your mind. This is the greatest and most important command. The second is like it: Love your neighbor as yourself. All the Law and the Prophets depend on these two commands."*

The lesson in these passages can be devastating: If your life isn't marked by love, then you don't know God. If you've been a Christian for a week or a decade and you aren't living more completely in love than you were a week or a decade ago, then perhaps you haven't actually come to know God.

The Christian life is about being transformed by God

I'm not talking about a bland repetition of the so-called sinner's prayer. I am not against the sinner's prayer, but there is a problem with it. It is a reduced view of what the gospel is and contains and communicates. Forming a relationship with the Almighty is more than signing a little card and parroting a prayer in the front row of a sanctuary. Typically, a sinner's prayer goes something like this:

"Dear Jesus, I admit that I am a sinner."

OK, that's good. I think that's important. That's central.

"I ask You to forgive me of my sin."

Forgiveness is crucial.

"I ask You to come into my heart and be my Savior and my Lord."

Good to put Him in His proper place.

But we have missed the fact that entering the Christian life is not simply praying the right words and signing a commitment card. To be a Christian is to be transformed by the God to whom we pray. And the God to whom we pray, according to the Bible, is love. So, ultimately, we do a disservice to people when we say, "Just pray this prayer," and then pronounce them *saved* or *born again* or whatever term is *en vogue* at the moment. A person can read a prayer and still experience none of those things. But when it is genuinely the intent of that person's heart to follow Christ, God transforms that person.

A religious act isn't what makes a person a Christian. Committing one's life to Christ in repentance and faith, being covered by His atoning sacrifice, receiving His forgiveness—that's when the transformation of new birth takes place. In other words, allowing Christ to take our place on the Cross and make peace for us is the love that accomplishes salvation in our lives. We are made Christ followers by His love, not by our effective prayer, impassioned by a stirring invitation and enunciated properly. As a Christ follower, my life should be evidenced by a different kind of life and a different kind of love. So what do you do now? Since you already sign your cards "Love, _____," it's about time to take that love on mission with us. The nature of the church, born out of the character of God, is missional *by nature,* and love stands guard over that mission.

We should begin by extending a compassionate heart to the members of our church. Whenever we feel prompted to check in with an absent member, we do it out of love instead of duty. This Sunday, we can sit somewhere different in the sanctuary and interact with an older person who often sits alone. When we sit down to dinner with our family this week, we can collectively decide who we are going to reach out to—perhaps someone in our church who is in pain. These simple acts of love will put us on the proper path to "carrying a cup of cold water in Jesus' name."

But we should also think beyond the people we see each Sunday morning for worship. Right now, decide to invite a family over for dinner who has never attended your church before. Contact your Bible study group today and plan on taking care packages to a home for abused women in the county. Take a look at a world map and realize that there are billions who have limited or zero access to the gospel. From the lonely in your community to the unreached people group on another continent, many are in need of God's love. There are a myriad of ways to go on mission with God and express His love to those who need it desperately.

As we become more like Christ, we demonstrate His love. Only by love's demonstration can the church accomplish its mission. God's character is the standard to live by, one which we will never meet fully. We may find some who will describe our congregations as loving, but we will never *be* love as "God *is* love." But as we become more like Christ, His love is demonstrated in us.

Remember, the demonstration of His love involved death. *"While we were still sinners, Christ died for us"* (Romans 5:8). We can both be loved and respond by love when we respond to His call to salvation in our lives. Becoming a Christian is the first and necessary step. If you have never surrendered your life to Christ and received Jesus' free gift of salvation, set this book aside and go to our Heavenly Father in prayer. Confess your sinfulness to Him, repent, and place your faith in Christ alone for salvation. As you respond to God's call to intimacy, He will bring you into a personal relationship with Him and make you a member of His church.

Many of us, however, have already responded to Christ's call and are believers. In that case, we should allow the Holy Spirit to take inventory of love's foundation in our lives and church. Without a doubt, conviction of our lack of love will follow. There is not a person holding this book who has fully lived out the measure of love God has for us and seeks for us to live in our lives.

So this is the moment to examine just how God's presence is being demonstrated in your life and in your church. Ask God to make you so marked by love that life becomes new again. May your church be different because God demonstrated His own love for you.

Points for Personal Reflection
and Group Discussion

1. How do you think other people honestly describe you? Is God's love a part of the description?

2. God desires to reveal Himself to you. What can you do to more intimately relate to Him? What spiritual practices will help you draw closer to Christ?

3. Read Acts 2:42–47. How are you and your church fulfilling the characteristics of the early church? What is your church known for in your community?

4. Meditate on the idea of your spiritual adoption by God. How does the metaphor of adoption describe God's love for the church?

5. Who do you know that would benefit from understanding the metaphor of God adopting us as His children?

6. Love is the standard for the identity of the church. How can your Bible study or missions group or you as an individual be on mission with God in a loving way to your community?

7. Are there areas in your life that could be described by the oxymoron of "unloving Christian?" How can you begin to change this way of life?

8. We are to both demonstrate and speak about the gospel of love. Which do you find easier and why? How can you begin to do the one that is more difficult for you?

Chapter 6

COMMISSIONED
BY LOVE

LIVING WITH JESUS' MISSION

We have seen that love is the very heart of God. Love does not govern God for that would make Him subject to something else. Rather, He has divinely chosen love as an expression of His character. In response to His love, what is the church supposed to do? The answer is found in His final instructions to His followers: make disciples

Each church is called to minister uniquely because the culture surrounding it is unique. Churches in the suburbs, rural areas, or beach towns each have unique cultures. But despite the cultural differences, the churches in those places share the common mission given by Christ. Christ's commission gives us certain principles that *all* churches must fulfill in *all* times and in *all* places because they are inherent to being the church. Though we are stationed in various fields of ministry, we share a common purpose.

The same is true for people. We have differing needs and interests. Some like to stay home and watch movies, while others participate in triathlons. Personally, I am not excited about running around for hours at a time, but that is another story—and the point is, we *all* have different likes and strengths. No matter your personal preference or hobby, there are still basic life functions everyone must fulfill. Shopping for groceries, caring for our homes, paying the bills, and so on. Some parts of life can be personalized, while others are compulsory for everyone.

In the final verses of Matthew's Gospel, Jesus gives a command that is for all churches at all times and in all cultures: the Great Commission. It is the missional call for the body of believers in general and individual believers in particular. Each church or group discovers specific ways to respond to its culture, but all churches make that response with certain foundational truths and practices. It reads:

Then Jesus came near and said to them, "All authority has been given to Me in heaven and on earth. Go, therefore, and make disciples of all nations, baptizing them in the name of the Father and of the Son and of the Holy Spirit, teaching them to observe everything I have commanded you. And remember, I am with you always, to the end of the age."

—MATTHEW 28:18–20

Generations of Christians before us have well noted that this passage is not known as the "OK Suggestion" or the "Afterthought of Jesus." Instead, it is a foundational direction for the church's work and character. It is the last word given to the church before Christ's ascension.

Behind and Before

Christ sends the apostles and early believers out to follow Jesus as He demonstrates and expands His kingdom. But it was not in the same vein as the expansion of the Roman Empire. God's kingdom is not defined by geography and politics. Rather, it displays itself wherever the reign of God exists in the human heart.

Before we move any further, we should note the provisions surrounding *"Go, therefore, and make disciples"* (v. 19). Christ begins the Commission by reminding us that *"all authority has been given to me in heaven and on earth"* (v. 18). Then He concludes by assuring us that *"I am with you always, to the end of the age"* (v. 20). Even as Christ sends the apostles and early believers out to do kingdom work, intimacy with God alone is sufficient for the work. Only God, who by His character loves, would not only make the assignment, but would invite us to join in the work He is already doing throughout creation. Let there be no mistake, He does not send us out alone; He reminds us of His prevailing presence in the work.

We offer a caution here: Missional ministry is not about having the coolest church or the most technologically savvy ministry. It is not simply a race to the finish line of "most contextualized." Many are witty enough to crack the culture, emotionally wedge in with people, and intellectually convince others of the truth. But missional ministry is not about our abilities. It is about presenting God's presence to the people of our world. If it becomes something besides that, then all we've done is create a new idol.

Many attempt to grow individual churches through "gimmicks," such as concerts, sermon series with shocking themes, special event days, or pastors shaving their heads if the high-attendance goal is reached. But here is the point: When we educate members and the public to attend our church based on attention-grabbing events, we are also educating them to attend other churches, nonprofit organizations, and even cults based on the events they offer. God's mission and true growth in a church is based on the loving authority of Christ, not imaginative gimmicks.

As Jesus began His ministry, Mark's Gospel describes this scene: *"After John was arrested, Jesus went to Galilee, preaching the good news of God: 'The time is fulfilled, and the kingdom of God has come near. Repent and believe in the good news!'"* (Mark 1:14–15). When Jesus states that the kingdom of God is near, He is referring to His own presence among them. As believers, we move forward in missional ministry as ambassadors of the King who travels with us by the Holy Spirit.

As we take a look at the Great Commission, there is a missional movement to this statement by Christ. And so we begin with the simple word: "Go."

A mission that moves

When Philip and his family moved to a new city, they joined a church and become Bible study teachers. In one season, his wife Angie and he took up the task of teaching a group of second graders for a year. With their sons now teenagers, they had forgotten (probably on purpose) just how "active" a second grader can be. He said that they would come into the room in a flurry, move non-stop for an hour, and then leave as active as they arrived. I think we need to take a cue from such small children. The command of Christ is to be up and moving.

In the original language of the New Testament, the word *go* is not about a particular destination. Literally translated, it means "as you are going." God has certain destinations for believers, but it's faulty thinking to put on blinders until we get there. Instead, we need to be prepared daily to carry the message of Christ to whomever we meet. We are a sent people, not a sedentary organization. As Christ's ambassadors, we do poorly when we try to close ourselves off from opportunities, and this includes secluding ourselves within our church community. The church must never lose the sense that we are sent. Staying at home base is not an option Christ gave us.

The "come-see-what-we-are-doing" attitude ruins the missional activity of the church. Certainly, the Lord made the simple call of "Come" to a number of people. But in just over three years, He gave them the permanent "Go." An "our-place-is-safer" attitude will separate us from the very people God sent us to. The command to "go" guards us against becoming the Evangelical Amish of the twenty-first century.

Perhaps you have attended church throughout childhood, been a leader in the youth group, and graduated from a Christian college. Perhaps those experiences prepared you for life and ministry. However, we must avoid creating the "bubble" that keeps us and our children from being able to befriend the lost. Instead, we need to find ways to keep going out among them.

When Philip needed a new cell phone, he started visiting one particular store. He did this because we need to go to the people who are not coming to us. At that store, he encountered three employees: a single mom, a married pregnant mom, and a stand-offish manager. The temptation was to get in, get the phone, and get out. Instead, God desired an intersection of the gospel with the people at the cell phone store. The single mom was interested in finding a place for her four-year-old to learn about God. The married woman, who was eight months pregnant, needed a church that met her needs. The manager—well, he was just too cool to talk about religious subjects. Philip could have found a more convenient store and spent less time on a phone purchase but he kept his focus on people rather than the conveniences of life. Only eternity will be able to tell what the simple conversations will bring.

Perhaps you should do the same. Instead of using a different gas station each week, go to the same station and begin chatting with the clerk. Or use the same checkout person at the grocery store. Go to lunch each week with that demanding person in the cubicle down the hall. Plan a backyard ice cream party for your neighbors this summer, and make sure that you invite that needy or difficult family on your block. We never know what our *going* may mean to others. It will show a level of love they have not witnessed from others. In other words, each of us must learn to be a friend—just as Christ has become a friend to us (John 15:14–15).

The example of Christ is for us to be *among those* in the world. Dinners with the sinful and the despised were characteristic of our Lord. Those whom the religious deemed as sinners were one thing, but to eat with a tax collector was even worse in their eyes. Jesus' visitation with these people was an extension of the heart of God. The hatred of the Pharisees only proved their mentality of law instead of love.

The disposition of the legalistic is to isolate. The passion of the missional is to engage.

It's interesting Jesus was most harsh with the religious people who isolated themselves from the world. Luke tells us about Jesus eating in the home of Simon the Pharisee (Luke 7:36–50). A sinful woman comes in to wash the feet of the Master with an expensive perfume. Simon is appalled at her presence but even more at Jesus' reaction to her. Simon thinks to himself, *"This man, if He were a prophet, would know who and what kind of woman this is who is touching Him—she's a sinner!"* (v. 39). Jesus confronted Simon with a lesson on forgiveness and love. He pointed out how Simon had been forgiven little and how that sinful woman had received great forgiveness. I look forward to meeting her some day in heaven; I hope Simon will be there as well.

The church must stop worrying about who is touching us. Certainly, we don't surrender to the moral quandary in which the world operates. But it's time for us to see people through the same lens God uses. We need the exaggerated passion Paul displays: *"For I could almost wish to be cursed and cut off from the Messiah for the benefit of my brothers, my own flesh and blood. They are Israelites, and to them belong the adoption, the glory, the covenants, the giving of the law, the temple service, and the promises"* (Romans 9:3–4). We will address more of this subject in chapter 12.

The Destination: Make Disciples

What are we to go and do? The central verb of Matthew 28:19 is "make" in the phrase "make disciples." Everything else we do in the mission of God should revolve around that activity.

Jesus did not say "make converts" or "teach them to pray a particular prayer." Rather, this is about people who are born again through the power of the Savior who died and rose again. You and I are to participate in the work of multiplying the number of surrendered learners and followers of Christ. We are to lead people into the kingdom by way of the Cross. Again, this is not about enrolling people into a Bible study group or making them an adherent to our particular denomination. Rather, they are to intimately follow Christ.

The use of the word *make* signals us to be involved in the process. Scripture describes believers in this way: *"Now we have this treasure in clay jars, so that this extraordinary power may be from God and not from us"* (2 Corinthians 4:7).

Today, clay jars are decorative items placed about the home to add color or panache. However, in the time of the early church, a clay pot was just a storage container. They were as common as the plastic tubs one buys at the dollar store. And yet diamonds can be stored in a cheap container. As the church, we are a collection of these plain vessels that carry the gospel. We bring the light of Christ to those in the dark, but we are just the instrument, not the light. We pour out the water of life to those who exist in a spiritual drought, but we are only the jar, not the water. We serve the bread of life to a famished soul, but we are only the plate, not the bread. We make disciples by intentionally carrying this message to the lost.

The church must go beyond being a Christian form of Dudley Do-Right in the community. We are emissaries of God's kingdom with a singular agenda. Remember, the word *missional* should describe the normal mode of the believer's life, living like a *missionary* at all times. Our lives must be more than being good neighbors and doing good things. Doing good is important to who we are, but it does not define us. Like a missionary, we are to contend for the faith, present Christ in a contextualized manner that can be received by the hearers, and operate in a countercultural community of faith. The end result of our very different mission is to persuade people of the greatness of Christ and His redemption (2 Corinthians 5:11).

In Matthew 28, Jesus is preparing His followers for His departure. This is the time for final instructions like what you leave with the babysitter when you go out. Notice what Jesus did not tell them to do. He did not say: "Go and be the very best neighbors in the community. Go and be excruciatingly moral. Go and get a good education. Go and raise nice children." He did say, *"Go and make disciples."*

The early church in Rome was struggling about what to believe and how to behave. The Apostle Paul reminded them of the role others played in their conversion and the role they must continue in.

> *But how can they call on Him they have not believed in? And how can they believe without hearing about Him? And how can they hear without a preacher? And how can they preach unless they are sent? As it is written: How beautiful are the feet of those who announce the gospel of good things!*
>
> —ROMANS 10:14–15

You and I did not come to Christ because it suddenly dawned on us. Rather, someone told us. God sent someone to tell us. Who are the people in your life who had a hand in your coming to salvation? Make a mental list of the family members, friends, and church workers who all played a role in God's voice calling to you. This is a great moment for you to thank our heavenly Father for graciously using those who loved you to bring you to Him.

Our central work is to make disciples. Second Peter 3:9 reflects God's heart: *"The Lord does not delay His promise, as some understand delay, but is patient with you, not wanting any to perish but all to come to repentance."* Through the power of the Cross our passion must align with His as we go out to make disciples and glorify God.

The Next Step: Baptize Them

The next portion of the Commission deals with baptism. Our best understanding of Christ's commission is that water baptism follows a person's confession of Christ as Lord. By leading a new disciple to baptism, we are helping this new disciple identify with Christ as his or her Lord.

Though puzzling to some, Christ Himself was baptized in Matthew 3. His baptism was not to show He had experienced conviction and repentance.

After all, He is perfect in holiness. Rather, it signaled to the world that He would be obedient to the Father. For believers, baptism is a public acknowledgment of an inward reality. It is the sign that we are surrendering our lives to a relationship with God through identification with the death, burial, and resurrection of Christ. Baptism is much more important than many people realize. We cannot be obedient to the Great Commission without baptism.

The time of baptism is also the visual profession of a believer that the "old man" has died and Christ is their life now. The Apostle Paul taught the early believers, *"Therefore we were buried with Him by baptism into death, in order that, just as Christ was raised from the dead by the glory of the Father, so we too may walk in a new way of life"* (Romans 6:4). We do not get wet in the church Jacuzzi just for the sake of being like everyone else. Baptism is like an arrow pointing to heaven, saying a death and a resurrection have occurred in a person's life.

Baptism is also, in a lesser measure, an identification with the church. Philip's favorite baptistery is at The Church at Brook Hills in Birmingham, Alabama. Instead of having the baptistery placed in the wall behind the choir loft, Brook Hills' sits in front of the platform area on the main floor of their worship room. This position allows for more intimacy with those who share in this profession of faith and celebrate this new life in Christ. The believer being baptized faces the church family. Coming up out of the water, the church erupts in celebration, as if the new believer has stepped off the sidewalk and into the parade of victory.

As missionaries to our community, we lead new disciples to be baptized for the good of many. All at once, baptism is a proclaiming love to God, a cry of solidarity with the church, and a witness to the community.

Repeating the Process: Teaching Them to Obey

We are all sinners, rogues by nature. Our children prove it. We never teach them to be selfish or to lie; they come by that naturally. The psalmist declared,

The fool says in his heart, "God does not exist." They are corrupt; they do vile deeds. There is no one who does good. The Lord looks down from heaven on the human race to see if there is one who

is wise, one who seeks God. All have turned away; all alike have become corrupt. There is no one who does good, not even one.

—PSALM 14:1–3

Therefore, when a person comes to Christ, the loving thing to do is teach that person how to follow his or her Lord—that teaching comes from God's inerrant Word, made transforming by the Spirit, lived out in the life of a growing believer. That is what it means to "teach them to observe" and to grow up in faith. It would be cruel to simply leave them in a state of infant faith; left to their own devices. There they will remain ignorant in their understanding and juvenile in their practice.

Colossians 3:5 gives the command that the new believer is to *"put to death what belongs to your worldly nature." The Message* phrases it as *"that means killing off everything connected with that way of death."* And what are we to execute? The verse goes on to list the sinful things that need to be put to death. We can't expect new believers to master these things alone. Just as children must be taught to do things for themselves, new believers must be taught to mature in setting aside selfishness. Though it may be difficult, it is necessary.

God requires us to kill, mortify, and execute our flesh that makes us feel *so good.* Remember from our chapter on Christ, death is heavily involved in love, but this is a not a natural perspective for human beings. For us, self-preservation is natural. Living out the mission of God means believers must teach and model for new Christians that death is the new form of love in our lives.

We teach disciples how to submit to God's commands and Christ's example. John 13 is a great starting point to boil that down into portions we can hand to new believers. Here we see Jesus modeling how we should serve. In those days, the lowest of servants in the household normally washed feet. When there was no servant present, the person arriving first would wash his own feet and then wash the feet of the next person arriving; in turn each person washed the feet of the one following them. As the 12 apostles gather for the Passover meal, apparently no one washes their own feet or anyone else's feet. So Jesus humbles

Himself and moves around the room, washing the feet of this unlikely group of followers.

It's usually not difficult to serve those who will serve us in return. But this is not the scene in which Christ is teaching. He washes the feet of those who will run into the night when He is arrested, of the one who will doubt His resurrection, and of the one who will curse at the accusation of knowing Jesus later that night. Jesus even washes the feet of the one who will betray Him. As Jesus serves Judas, we see an amazing example of humility. This is a great place for us to begin, by teaching people the nature of Christ in His service.

When Philip was a young man entering the ministry, his good friend Matt Roskam taught him of the two bowls of water at the end of Jesus' life. First is the bowl of water used by Jesus in John 13. It is the bowl of humble love poured out for others. The second bowl is quite different. It is the one used by Pilate. *"When Pilate saw that he was getting nowhere, but that a riot was starting instead, he took some water, washed his hands in front of the crowd, and said, 'I am innocent of this man's blood. See to it yourselves!'"* (Matthew 27:24). This one is the bowl of indifference, selfishness, and arrogance. It is the bowl that released the criminal Barabbas, rather than care about the blood of an innocent man.

As believers, we choose from two bowls every day. It is certainly a choice moved by love—either love for God and others or love for self. Teaching new disciples to serve with the loving humility of Christ is an appropriate lesson as they begin their new life.

New disciples should also learn the lesson of fruit. Jesus weaves the idea of obedience, love, and fruit into one of His final lessons.

As the Father has loved Me, I have also loved you. Remain in My love. If you keep My commands you will remain in My love, just as I have kept My Father's commands and remain in His love. I have spoken these things to you so that My joy may be in you and your joy may be complete. This is My command: Love one another as I have loved you. No one has greater love than this, that someone would lay down his life for his friends.

You are My friends if you do what I command you. I do not call you slaves anymore, because a slave doesn't know what his master is doing. I have called you friends, because I have made known to you everything I have heard from My Father. You did not choose Me, but I chose you. I appointed you that you should go out and produce fruit and that your fruit should remain, so that whatever you ask the Father in My name, He will give you.
This is what I command you: Love one another.

—JOHN 15:9–17

Obviously, the lessons of this passage alone could span an entire book. But here we see the need to help new believers understand that their new relationship with Christ is one of insight and reproduction. The mission of God is to reach them with redemption but does not end with their salvation. We are saved out of His love, and now we are to be active in Christ's mission as well. New believers naturally want to do this. So while we are teaching a new disciple to obey, we should allow his or her excitement to teach us again about the urgency of helping others come to Christ.

This lesson ends with the idea of going. We *go* because He appoints us to go bear fruit out of our love for Him. By obeying Him and His commands, we will remain in His love. If we obey, He can appoint us to bear fruit for the kingdom. In turn, those who are the new fruit in God's household go out and, by loving obedience, bear more fruit. This teaching of love, obedience, death, and fruit guides us to constantly go with Him in His work. It is a cycle that should be forever present in our lives.

If you didn't know this before, you need to go and make disciples. Consider yourself commissioned!

When asked what the purpose of the church is, too many of us give a self-serving answer: fellowship, ministry to the members (i.e., me), and pastoral counsel. It's a tragedy when a church becomes satisfied with who it already has, without regard for who else it might reach for Christ. We must guard against the onset of the "holy huddle" mentality that, in effect, says the rest of the world can perish.

In the summer of 2007, Christina (one of the new believers from the church where Philip and I served together) and her family went out of state to visit some friends for a week. Since Sunday morning worship was their practice at home, they accompanied the family's children to a local church nearby.

The church was small and it was obvious that Christina's family was visiting. During the service, the pastor spoke about an upcoming national denominational meeting that would advocate a change in how churches conducted evangelistic outreach. He opposed any such change. What worked in generations past should be good enough for the lost today. At the end of his diatribe, his final words shocked and crushed Christina's heart: "The church is not here for the lost."

Just a year earlier, Christina had been the lost person for whom this pastor now said change wasn't necessary. She was the one who would not have come naturally—ever—to a church like his. Why? Because she needed a place where people would love her as God does in order for her to see the gospel. So, with love as the main strategy for reaching out, our church used various methods to reach her and lead her to a vibrant faith in Christ. After coming to Christ, she had a deep desire to be baptized and learn how to follow Christ. But this leader had just told his church that she had not been worth the effort.

We believe the church's purpose is to glorify God, not to make people happy. The church does not exist for believers or unbelievers; it exists for God's glory, for the equipping of believers, and the church is God's missionary in the world. G. Campbell Morgan puts it succinctly when writing about Jesus' High Priestly Prayer (John 17): "The deepest passion of the heart of Jesus was not the saving of men, but the glory of God; and then the saving of men, because that is for the glory of God."[1] We exist and work to bring others to a reconciled position with God so there will be more people to love and honor Him.

If we believers are not actively honoring God by multiplying the number of followers He has—then we must repent! Since the church is alive, it should bear fruit. If you find yourself in a quagmire of rebellion, then choose to turn back to the One who forgives and restores. As the Apostle John reminded us, if we are to remain in His love, then we must obey His commands. We may fail. After all, we are just cheap plastic tubs holding diamonds, but we must not be deterred from our loving work for the Father. Let's go!

Points for Personal Reflection
and Group Discussion

1. What is the central mission that Jesus gave to the church?

2. What difference does it make for God's presence and authority to be with the church to fulfill the Great Commission? How does His presence affect our everyday lives and our work to intentionally go out to the lost?

3. Discuss how you, your group, or your church can *go* and engage your community in a way that can bring people to a better understanding of the gospel.

4. How does Philip's story of connecting with unbelievers at the cell phone store help you to identify some opportunities you can take advantage of?

5. What have been some effective means of making disciples in your community? What new ideas can you and your group or church begin to implement?

6. Share how your experience with baptism services have encouraged your faith and expressed it to others.

7. Discuss some of the basic lessons all new believers should be taught.

8. Think of a new believer in Christ who is in your church or circle of friends. How could you help him or her learn to obey Christ's teachings?

Chapter 7

DIRECTED BY LOVE

GIVING UP ON OUR "NEEDS"

His bulging veins and trembling hands preceded his words. He'd listened until he couldn't take it anymore; and as he spoke, his voice escalated until he was almost yelling. What had gotten this man, a brother in Christ, so upset?

I was speaking to a group of Anglicans, former Episcopalians really, when I was interrupted by the older gentlemen. I was training the group in starting Anglican churches. Teaching on church planting is not new to me, but I always try to tailor my talk to the people I am speaking to, so I spoke about the need to plant a biblically faithful and culturally relevant church in the culture receiving the church. I explained that the how of ministry is in many ways determined by the who, when, and where of culture.

I made a point of describing that every group must search the Scriptures and come to the conclusion of what a biblical church is. That conclusion is the group's best understanding of the biblical truth of church. That then becomes the group's biblical *tradition* (in the positive sense of the word). And, I explained, that, as Anglicans, the churches this group would plant would have a bigger *T* in their tradition than mine would. As a "low-church" evangelical, I am part of a denomination that does not have liturgical worship services or a strict hierarchy for church leadership. But the church is a big family and we need everyone to engage in God's mission.

We talked a bit about what a biblically faithful Anglican church must have, according to their understanding of the Scriptures. They listed things like the Eucharist, confession of sin, readings of Scripture, and so on. Then, I asked, "If that is what is required, what about the rest—how do you choose so many other issues, from music, to dress, to time of worship, etc.?"

They concluded, perhaps with a little promotion on my part, that these issues would be determined by *where* they were planting this Anglican church. So, I asked, "Is a traditional Anglican church OK?" "Sure." "Is a contemporary one OK?" "Sure." "What about one that had no building, stained glass, altar guild, etc., etc.?" They went along for a while . . . until he could take it no more.

"But that would not be a real Episc— I mean, Anglican church," the gentleman practically yelled, trembling and upset. "I left the Episcopal Church because they were changing things, and I want a church that feels right."

The tension was thick, he was ticked, and everyone wanted to know what I, someone from outside of their tradition, would say.

But, the answer was surprisingly easy. These Anglicans, seeking to be on a missional journey, found an ally. Because of Anglican theology, you can't really be an Anglican unless you have a bishop who traces ordination all the way back to the apostles. (Long story, but it is important to them.) So, they had to find a bishop who believed what they believed and would provide pastoral care for them—ordain their priests, plant new churches, and lead them in Christ's mission.

So, these Anglicans came "under" an archbishop from Africa. I was privileged to meet Archbishop Kolini, the African archbishop of Rwanda who provides spiritual oversight to these believers. I was so encouraged to hear his passion for the church and the gospel. I am glad to have him as a brother in the kingdom of God.

And, he was the spiritual authority over my upset friend. So, I asked, "How do you feel about how your archbishop worships at his church?" Ultimately, so many of our arguments about style and preferences collapse when we cross cultures. Again, in many ways, the how of ministry is determined by the who, when, and where of culture.

Where we are matters

Painfully, for my friend who was so agitated by the discussion of adjusting our ministry methods, the culture inside the church was the priority. How he was raised, his preferences, and what he missed determined ministry. He longed for the smells and bells of his former church. What he missed is what he loved. And he is not the only one. It is hard for people to hear that our stateside churches need to be relevant to the culture. Our approach, even stateside, should be like that of missionaries, where the essentials of our faith are never altered, but the how of ministry is adjusted according to the who, when, and where of the congregation.

In other words, if you have two congregations, both teaching the same timeless message, but one is in inner-city Chicago and the other in Tokyo, how would you choose on *less essential* issues, such as dress, time of worship, music, etc.? The group's consensus seemed to be that the location of each church should determine those issues

In *Breaking the Missional Code,* David Putman and I wrote:

> One of the most important considerations in breaking
> the code is to break from our own preferences.
> Simply put, being missional does not mean doing
> things the way we like them. It means to take the
> gospel into the context where we have been called
> . . . and to some degree, to let the church take the
> best shape it can in order to reach a specific culture.
> However, the problem is our preferences. You
> can't be missional and pick what you like at the
> same time.

Yet, if love compels us, shouldn't we, in love, willingly set aside our own preferences in order to reach others?

Love people, not preferences

Churches can (and do) fight to the death (sometimes literally) over their preferences. You can preach heresy at a lot of churches, and people will not object. Leaders can lead double lives, and people will let it be. But, change the order of service, and it's time for a fight.

We love the wrong things. We miss what we love about our church's culture. Actually, the fact that we love *things* may be the whole problem. *We need to love people.* We tend to think of "our" traditions as being biblical and other traditions as extrabiblical or nonbiblical. If we'd spend this energy and passion on the lost, our communities would likely be transformed for Christ sooner than we would expect.

Around the world, we teach missionaries to take the gospel into different cultures. We train them to love people, to love the culture of those people, and to give themselves away to them.

One of my friends, Jack, helped as I wrote this book. Jack and his family serve overseas in a place I cannot name. After more than 25 years of ministry in the US, he left a high-level denominational position to live in a country that does not allow missionaries. He and his family are learning a new language, embracing a new culture, and learning to love people who are very different than themselves. His family's decision illustrates how love compels us to give up the familiar in order to take the gospel wherever we are called.

Love others enough to babble like a baby

Jack explains why his and his wife's, Jesse's, love for God enables them to love people in a country far from home:

"I loved serving in the US. However, during several short-term trips, I was introduced to the overwhelming needs of a particular country in East Asia. This country has more than 40 cities with populations of a million people with no known evangelical presence. Because of these experiences, I was forced to reconsider my ministry career. I 'thought' I was compelled by love to go; however, I have since realized that I *am* now compelled by love to stay. Some days are very difficult; yet a genuine love for God and His world compels me to continue our ministry.

"When I first considered this change in my family's life, I thought, *How hard could it be?* I was a seasoned minister. I had 25 years of experience. I had been a leader on the local, associational, state, and national level. But, when I arrived in my new city and found myself waiting outside the restroom doors of a local restaurant for someone to come out so I would know which door to go in, I was completely humbled.

"I quickly realized I had two choices. First, I could refuse to adapt and spend the bulk of my time witnessing to the people in my city that speak a minimal amount of English (at most a few hundred university students), or I could change. It would mean spending countless hours in a classroom and at first 'babbling like a baby,' but I knew that only by adapting to the culture and language of this foreign country would I really be able to share the gospel with the vast majority of people that live here.

"It has been difficult! Since I am from the rural mountains of middle Tennessee, I feel that I learned English as a second language! However, as my family has adjusted ourselves to this culture, God was already at work, and we are beginning to see miracles that we used to only read about in missions magazines!

"Please continue to pray for us as we attempt to share the love of God with people in their own heart language."

"Babbling like a baby." That phrase reminds me of Christ's incarnation. He humbled Himself and became like us. God the Son moved out of the eternal throne room for a time and stepped into the womb of an ordinary Jewish girl. Jesus came down and spoke our language, but even He had to learn it first as a child. On His mission, Christ was willing to live in our neighborhood, eat our food, and learn our language in order to reach us.

Missionaries are as Jack describes. We intentionally teach them how to understand a different culture and how to minister in this new setting. And we celebrate when they do. But, did you know vocational missionaries want us to do the same? They hope that we will intentionally work to understand our current culture and learn how to minister in communities that have radically changed over the last few decades. Jack wrote specifically for *us* this letter about his family's mission experience.

"I am not sure I look, act, or feel much like a missionary. The pictures I remember from missionary speakers in the late 60s and early 70s (mud huts with mosquito nets) are very different than the way my family currently lives overseas today (air-conditioning and Internet with Skype). Instead, we are choosing to live here in the same manner that we lived in the US, missionally (missions-minded).

"This should be true for you, too, even if you live in North America. Let me give you an example. When we graduated from seminary in 1987, my wife and I moved to northern Michigan to plant a church. When we arrived in the small town of 4,000 (five hours north of Detroit), we found it was mostly inhabited by people from Polish and German heritages. We quickly realized that 'all Caucasian people are not alike.' Even within the US, northerners and southerners have different ways of doing and seeing things. We immediately began to adapt our church planting skills to better relate to people from a different background than us.

"Let me give you another example. I grew up in Tennessee in a rural, isolated community. There were no 'foreigners' in our community. Today, there is a Spanish-speaking radio station, two Hispanic grocery stores, and a hotel owned by people from East Asia. And these don't even include all the foreigners . . . well, northerners, who are moving to this beautiful southern setting in order to retire. My parents have to look at their home town like I look at my new setting. They must see it as a missions field.

"Oddly, they are learning that even the people who were born and grew up in their community are not the same as they were 50 years ago. The 'natives' now have high-speed Internet, satellite TV, and XM radio in their tractors! Even among the locals, they must see their community as a missions field.

"So, my parents' church has two options. First, they could require people to dress like them, talk like them, and think like them before they're welcome at church. Or, they can learn to adapt to a new culture and maybe even learn a 'new' language. The first option is the easiest. However, it may mean the death of their church. The second option is much more difficult. It requires change.

"What would make a church change a hundred years of traditions? The only answer is love. If we love the people who live where God placed us, we will do what it takes to reach them. Love compels us to become all things to all people, so that by all means we may reach some."

Jack's letter challenges us to live in a different way from just bland religious activisim. Instead his encouragement to us is to consider where we live—we need to really understand the culture of our community. But to do so, we need to know who lives around us. If we are going to be ambassadors to a neighborhood, city, or country, then we need to know who lives there, how they live, and their values. But, like Jack, we need to have a love for them as well. It is one thing to understand the demographics of a community and quite another to love the people behind the factoids. We need to learn from missionaries like Jack.

Living as missionaries live

Most Christians love missionaries; we love missions; we're even willing to financially support missions. Unfortunately, we love missionaries, but we don't really want to *be* like them. If we did, our churches would look less like *what we want* and more like *what God would want* as we adapt to reach the people in the culture around us.

Every Christmas, in my denomination, we give to an offering for missions work that is named after Lottie Moon, a woman who gave her life to reach the Chinese people for Jesus. She dressed in Chinese clothes, lived in the Chinese culture, and ate Chinese food—at least until she starved to death giving it all away. It is an immense irony that one of the greatest missionary examples in history is not the model in our own churches. Even as we think about local ministry, we should be asking, "What did Lottie Moon do?" We will not reach the North America of the twenty-first century for Christ if we continue to try to do so with the church methods that worked in the North America of the 1950s. The Apostle Paul taught:

> *To the weak I became weak, in order to win the weak. I have become all things to all people, so that I may by every possible means save some. Now I do all this because of the gospel, so I may become a partner in its benefits.*
>
> —1 CORINTHIANS 9:22–23

These verses have been taught and preached so often that they've lost their meaning in our lives. So let me suggest another of Paul's challenges—"*For I could almost wish to be cursed and cut off from the Messiah for the benefit of my brothers, my own flesh and blood. They are Israelites*" (Romans 9:3–4).

Paul is using what our high school teachers taught us as *hyperbole*. It is when you make an outlandish statement in order to prove a point (like when our child says, "I'm starving to death" when all they need is a snack). Paul's passion is so great that not only is he willing to become all things to all people, he is willing to sacrifice a great amount so that those he loves will come to understand the gospel.

Yet for many of us in our churches, we cannot even give up our own Sunday morning preferences in order that men and women might be saved. It's a minor inconvenience to attend a church where you don't necessarily like the style. But when God is using it *and you* to reach the community, it is a privilege to show our love for God and our love for the community in that manner. What is really sad is when we attack sisters and brothers, who are not even in our congregations, for living out their faith in the way they believe God has told them. We should be very careful about criticizing other Bible-believing congregations for worshipping according to God's call upon them.

After all, it is love that inspires us to be different. Philippians 2:5 teaches us to "make [our] own attitude that of Christ Jesus."

JOY—Jesus. Others. You.

As a new believer in youth group, I learned the acronym JOY—**J**esus. **O**thers. **Y**ou. This meant: Jesus first; then others; then self.

It took me a little while to realize that many of the people in my congregation really didn't live like that, and it took even longer for me to own up to the fact that I didn't live like that either.

If Christ's love compels us, then Philippians 2 shows us the attitude we're compelled to develop: We're to think of others before we think of ourselves. This is a passage that forces us to face our sin: We love what we love more than we love other people. Paul says all that will change as the love of Christ compels us:

If then there is any encouragement in Christ, if any consolation of love, if any fellowship with the Spirit, if any affection and mercy,

*fulfill my joy by thinking the same way, having the same love,
sharing the same feelings, focusing on one goal.*

—PHILIPPIANS 2:1–2

In general, the Bible tells us to do things we aren't doing that we should be doing. Or, to stop doing the things we naturally do that we shouldn't be doing, so we can do new things under God's supernatural power. That's why Paul continues: *"Do nothing out of rivalry or conceit, but in humility consider others as more important than yourselves. Everyone should look out not only for his own interests, but also for the interests of others"* (Philippians 2:3–4).

There it is. That's love. That's love lived: thinking about others more than you think about yourself. It teaches us to live for the interest of others instead of our own. It is written not as an academic exercise, but to show us how to live within our congregations and within our communities. Paul wrote it as a letter to the believers in Philippi, but God intends it as a letter to all believers throughout history.

Yet, living with this missional attitude is impossible unless we're obedient to the compelling love of Christ. Think about it—fighting for our needs, preferences, and desires in church are common enough to be called normal. We too often battle for what we want rather than ask what would be best to reach the community.

In 2009, I served as the interim pastor of a large church in Nashville that had encountered great difficulty. I asked Philip to work on staff with me during the interim period. One of the odder occurrences happened when we were picketed . . . by another church. Nashville had suffered a horrible flood and, in the process of the church's finding a new identity, our congregation became very active in ministering to those whose homes were destroyed. A particular church that prides itself in pronouncing God's hatred toward sin and stating that every disaster is God's judgment decided to picket us on a Sunday morning.

It was a pitiful site. Rather than take up tools and grace to help the people in our city, they stood on the street with signs and pride. It was a moment that solidified in my mind the need to care more about the mission of God rather than the opinions of human judgment. No matter the level of our efforts, we will fall short of God's mission if we care more about our opinions than we do Christ's example.

Jesus empties Himself

Yet, the Scriptures say we should make our attitude like that of Jesus Christ (Philippians 2:5).[1] Jesus willingly chooses the path of humble service. Instead of telling us that we must simply be good, get along, and compromise, the Bible displays a servitude which can only be accomplished through the supernatural power of God.

I have often wondered what it must be like to be a mother, especially at dinnertime. Many moms rarely eat a hot meal. At best it is lukewarm. And why? Because they have set their preference for a hot meal aside in order to serve everyone else's food first. The one person in the house who has probably worked the hardest for the meal will probably receive the least pleasure from eating it. But I am reminded that moms do not cook so that they can enjoy. They cook so their family can enjoy.

Our heavenly Father sent His Son to work on earth. Jesus traded the residence of glory and the benefits of sitting upon His majestic throne for living in an arid landscape and a construction job. All of this was so the benefit of intimacy with God could be offered to us.

If God would require His Son to surrender so much, do not be surprised if He requires us to give up some of our rights or to restrict some of our preferences in order to reach those who still don't know Jesus.

This passage held such significance to the early church that they sang it as a hymn so everyone would continually remember: *"Make your own attitude that of Christ Jesus"* (Philippians 2:5). Paul goes on to explain that Jesus did not consider Himself but emptied and humbled. He was obedient to death so that His death would bring the Father glory (Philippians 2:6–11).

Jesus Others You. Indeed.

Imagine how different our churches would be if people asked, "If we did this in our church, would Jesus get the glory and would others be reached?" When that happens, we have a different kind of church. It is the type of church where we are *"thinking the same way, having the same love, sharing the same feelings, focusing on one goal"* (see Philippians 2:2). When that happens, we shine like lights in the world:

For it is God who is working in you, enabling you both to desire and to work out His good purpose. Do everything without grumbling and arguing, so that you may be blameless and pure, children of God who are faultless in a crooked and perverted generation, among whom you shine like stars in the world.

—PHILIPPIANS 2:13–15

Why is it that those who have been in the church longest are often the ones who are the most resistant to change for others? Can we instead say, "Here I am, Lord, send me" instead of Moses' statement, "Here am I, send Aaron"?

My Anglican friend was pretty upset when I challenged him. But, we talked. I asked him, "Do you think your archbishop (who, by the way, is an African in Rwanda) worships the same way you do?" He said, "No." I asked him, "Do you think he is being biblically faithful where God has placed him?" He replied immediately, "Yes."

We should encourage one another to find out what a biblically faithful and culturally relevant church would look like in our community, and be the first to say, "Send me."

Points for Personal Reflection and Group Discussion

1. For those of you who grew up attending church, what was the most puzzling tradition you remember? If you are new to attending church, what confused you at first?

2. Discuss the song lyrics or traditions in your current church that might confuse people in your community.

3. Describe the people of your community whom the Lord has called your church to reach for the gospel. What is the primary ethnic make-up, economic status, and religious background of your community? When you think about who lives there, what do they care about most?

4. How has your community changed over the last decade?

5. What would a biblically faithful, culturally relevant church look like in the place where your church is located? Think about communication style, ministries offered, and involvement in the community events as starting points.

6. What barriers in your life do you perceive hinder the JOY attitude?

7. Describe what your group or church could give up in order to better make disciples in your community.

8. Philippians 2:14 teaches that we are to live without grumbling and arguing. How will this verse help in working through adjustments to our missional ministry in the community?

Chapter 8

SENT TO LOVE

DELIVERING
WHAT THE WORLD NEEDS MOST

The house was in terrible shape. In fact, most of the kids at the elementary school told stories that it was haunted. Every day, Philip drove past it on his way to appointm ents. The front porch did not look safe, shrubbery was unkempt, windows broken, and, he admits, it did look spooky. But then something amazing happened—someone bought that old house. Not only did they buy it, they also began to work on it. It took almost a year, but now it is beautiful and Philip is looking for an excuse to go by and take a closer look.

When someone puts their mind to making an impact, the results are often better than we hoped for in the beginning. No one thought that old house would be truly transformed. But we should never dismiss what a craftsman can do. A true artisan can turn around a dilapidated structure.

In *Comeback Churches*, I studied 324 churches that had experienced significant turnaround from decline and near death. We asked these pastors and leaders from ten different denominations, What happened that led to a revitalized church?

In chapter 2 of *Comeback Churches*, I focused on three faith factors that were commonly cited by these comeback leaders. They were

Factor 1: Renewed Belief in Jesus Christ and the Mission of the Church

Factor 2: Renewed Attitude for Servanthood

Factor 3: Strategic Prayer Efforts

Loving what is lesser

We found it most interesting that so many leaders told us their churches experienced a renewed attitude for servanthood. In *Comeback Churches*, we explained it as "loving what is lesser."

"Comeback leaders led their members to care more about their communities than their preferences. Churches will split over preferences—without either side caring about the lost. Comeback Churches have decided that the 'sin of preferences' leads to the 'sin of a dying church.' This is particularly true when a culture changes so quickly.

"Internationally-known church consultant Lyle Schaller frequently asks the same question when beginning to consult with a church. The question speaks to every church today. Lyle asks, 'What year is it here?' Every church is living in some era. The issue is whether the era within a church aligns with the reality of the era where the gospel needs to be proclaimed.

"Silver Dollar City is an amusement park in Branson, Missouri, and a cultural phenomenon to behold. Inside the park is a log cabin chapel. It's a fun place to sing and stomp. The songs are from an era long gone. It is a great place to see how people worshiped in that era. Yet, much of Silver Dollar City is preserved culture, not today's culture. It is not a presentation of the Gospel that would readily be accepted in Houston or Hartford. For too many, their churches are museums of past cultures no longer relevant in the world today.

"Every church should function in such a way that it can live in and reach people in contemporary culture. Comeback Churches accept this truth and act on it, and it's not just about music. Being contemporary to our culture will mean different styles in different communities. If we choose not to serve our community as it exists, what's the alternative? We are then making a choice to function by our own preferences and the internal cultures which we create. Sadly, churches that serve their preferences and church culture do not reach the unchurched and will not experience comebacks. It takes a servant spirit to not focus on your preferences."

The reality is too many of us love our preferences more than we love Christ's mission. Too often, this shows in our churches. It shows us when we hold on to our preferences in church and let go of our passion for lost people. When given the choice, most churches choose traditions over their own children. Rather than adjust the methods of our ministries to reach a new generation, we ask the generation to adjust to the methods suited for a time that has passed. But when we have every right (after all it's "our church"), when we have always done it that way (no reason to change if we like it), and when we are in prominent positions (we have earned it), we can easily make it about us.

How can we show the love we speak of here? We, and our churches, have to go—see ourselves as sent—and to act accordingly.

After declaring Himself "sent" 40 times in the Gospel of John alone, Jesus then reminds us *"Just as the Father has sent Me, I also send you"* (John 20:21). We are sent on mission for God's purposes to people in culture.

When they came to Mysia, they tried to go into Bithynia, but the
Spirit of Jesus did not allow them. So, bypassing Mysia, they came
down to Troas. During the night a vision appeared to Paul:
A Macedonian man was standing and pleading with him, 'Cross
over to Macedonia and help us!' After he had seen the vision,
we immediately made efforts to set out for Macedonia,
concluding that God had called us to evangelize them.

—ACTS 16:7–10

"Cross over to Macedonia and help us!" (v. 9). That simple phrase describes a passion lived in the life of Paul and modeled in the New Testament. "Come over and help us" begins to describe for us the kind of mission Paul felt he had, and we have, been given.

Cross over

We need a resurgence of Great Commission living in our churches and among God's people. To have it, we will need an equal revival of Great Commandment loving as well. We should see that John 3:16 (*"For God loved the world in this way: He gave His One and Only Son)"* leads us to John 20:21: *"As the Father has sent Me, I also send you."* The words of Jesus mean we are to "live sent," focused on God's mission, on God's purposes.

We can get more from the context. It says: *"Paul and his companions traveled throughout the region of Phrygia and Galatia, having been kept by the Holy Spirit from preaching the word in the province of Asia"* (Acts 16:6 NIV). Then they went to Mysia's border and tried to enter Bithynia, unsuccessfully. So they passed by Mysia and went down to Troas.

For the sake of your sanity, I will dispense with the geography lesson, but needless to say they were struggling and confused with their direction, which is something we all struggle with occasionally. Despite uncertainty, they couldn't stop going. They couldn't stop being compelled by love. They couldn't stop pressing forward for the cause of the gospel. They were going; they liked going. It was part of who they were.

We don't know how they were forbidden to enter these places. Was it a vision, a check in their spirit? No reason is given. It is nevertheless a wonderful statement of God's love for the Macedonian people that He goes to such lengths to ensure a gospel witness to them.

Cross over is an important phrase. Paul was speaking of Macedonia, but I think the example here gives us insight for our own context. When Paul heard the call there, he went to people in a community. That was his pattern. It's worthwhile to open to Acts and observe how Paul went in:

• He went to Pisidian Antioch and engaged a Jewish cultural context (Acts 13).

• He engaged a pagan cultural context in Lystra (Acts 14).

• He engaged high Greek culture with the gospel of Jesus Christ (Acts 17).

Notice how he went and engaged them in their context in each place. He did not go into pagan Lystra and try to discuss philosophy. They were simply people living in the outskirts of the empire. Philosophical arguments would have been of little help. But in a place such as Mars Hill, philosophical discussions had a great impact for the gospel. Based on Paul's action and pattern, it's not just a geographic "Cross over" that we see, but also a cultural one.

Philip once traveled to Athens, Greece on a missions trip with a group of college students. While there, he led a worship service and preached on Mars Hill. It is a rocky spot that sits halfway between the Parthenon and a valley once filled with ancient idols. The Parthenon was a temple dedicated to the Greek goddess Athena, and Mars Hill was a place of debate and legal hearings.

Many of his friends asked if he preached the same sermon delivered by Paul on that day in Acts 17. But that would have done no good. Paul engaged the culture from that hill that was present at the moment—Greek, religious, and logical. Philip was speaking to a group of believing college students participating in a mission trip. Paul had gone to that city to preach to those who were unbelievers. Philip was leading a group to do the same. They had both gone to the same spot on the Earth but both had unique hearers in that place. Whomever we find ourselves facing when ministry occurs should be the determining factor in how we minister. Paul, facing cynical unbelievers, gave a defense of the gospel. Philip, leading students on a mission trip, encouraged them to have confidence in the gospel they were proclaiming in a foreign land.

We, and our churches, must engage the culture here and now. Pining away for a culture of times past and the practices that are meaningful to us but are ineffective in reaching those around us is a selfish way to view the ministry of the church. Instead, we must engage the culture with the life-changing, unchanging message of Jesus Christ—even if we must set aside our preference to stay home and simply enjoy church as it has always been.

"Cross over and help"

One little word—"Cross over and *help*"—but it matters.

Lots of people have a poor understanding of what the word *help* means. Half of its usages in the New Testament refer to the act of God in salvation or some other saving act. Modern understanding of *help* has confused it. The mission of Jesus leads us to help the poor by providing shelter, the addict by aiding in recovery, and the grieving by offering counsel. These are all immensely helpful acts.

Yet, it is essential we remember that the most important step in helping anyone is introducing them to Jesus Christ. We should offer a proclamation of the gospel that communicates it well and a demonstration of the gospel that illustrates it with a changed life. Our mission must be tied into the mission of Jesus, to seek and save those who are lost! That's the mission of Jesus; that's the mission God has called us to: "Come over and *help* us." Since Paul went to preach, it's obvious the passage refers to helping by presenting the unchanging gospel. That's what matters—what matters most.

What does this reveal about help? It reminds us of one of the key "compelled by love" passages.

> *Therefore, because we know the fear of the Lord, we seek to*
> *persuade people. [...] We are not commending ourselves to you*
> *again. [...] For if we are out of our mind, it is for God; if we have*
> *a sound mind, it is for you. For Christ's love compels us, since we*
> *have reached this conclusion: If One died for all, then all died.*
> *[...] Everything is from God, who reconciled us to Himself through*
> *Christ and gave us the ministry of reconciliation: [...] and He has*
> *committed the message of reconciliation to us.*
>
> —2 CORINTHIANS 5:11, 12, 13–14, 18, 19

The help we offer is Jesus, who is the same yesterday, today, and forever. It is a privilege to live and act as agents of reconciliation. After all, we are joining Jesus in His mission, and that mission is to save the lost (Luke 19:10) and to serve the hurting (Luke 4:18–19).

"Cross over and help us"

This little pronoun *us* is essential to understanding the text. Luke is reporting the vision under the inspiration of the Holy Spirit and includes this important pronoun. He doesn't say, "Come and preach." He doesn't say, "Come and debate theology." He doesn't say, "Come and create a pious subculture." He doesn't say, "Come and change the laws." He says, "Come over and help us!" This requires investing in the lives of those we are to help.

We should do what it takes so men and women hear the gospel, not just preach to and against the culture they live in. That's hard because too many of us love our preferences (and preferred vision of culture) more than lost people.

Luke records Paul's reaction to the call from God: *"We immediately made efforts to set out for Macedonia, concluding that God had called us to evangelize them"* (Acts 16:10). Luke reiterates they were going to deliver the gospel to "them." When we keep ministry personal, then love drives us to effective delivery systems. If we ignore the humans to whom we are taking the gospel,

CHAPTER 8

we mope through the city like Jonah and then plant ourselves on a ridge waiting for God to smite them. Not really loving them—just fulfilling a religious duty.

The view of "us" becomes an undeniable fact of everyday life when you plant a church. Philip describes church planting as "close-quarter combat." We look into the eyes of people every day who are apathetic, and sometimes opposed, to the gospel. There is no avoiding these people when we are knocking on doors, visiting business leaders, and meeting other parents at the baseball field.

But the same is true of all of our ministries, whether you are a member or leader in the church. The ministry of crossing over to those who need the help of the gospel is given to each of us without exception. We do our ministry eye-to-eye with people. It is necessary to not just cross over into their community but to get into their lives. We are called to live among and for a group of people, not just in their faceless city.

Love drives missional ministry to be incarnate, next door to people who need it so desperately. God's Spirit pounds the need of our lost neighbors upon us as an ironsmith pummels an anvil. The faces of those who passed through our worship service only once are etched in our mind because we understand their eternal fate better than they do. Love for the glory and fame of Christ intensifies when we meet with a new friend and that person offers his or her life to Christ for the forgiveness of sin. "Us" connecting to Christ is what begins to make our heart beat in the morning.

Contending and Contextualizing

The Scriptures call us to *"contend for the faith"* (Jude 3). *Contending* is most decidedly an apt description. The Greek word behind "contend" means "to exert oneself without distraction to attain a goal. . . . Jude implies that the members of the church must exert themselves in spreading the gospel and defeating heresy." [Simon J. Kistemaker, *New Testament Commentary: James, Epistles of John, Peter, and Jude*. Grand Rapids, MI: Baker Academic, 1987, 372.] We must take seriously what the Bible teaches and live it out in our lives—and that is not always popular.

The Scriptures also call us to contextualize. That means we are to live out the gospel in different contexts, and that looks different from place to place. We already do this in the different Bible studies in our churches. You would never dream of teaching a group of fourth graders the same way you teach married couples in their forties or senior adult women in their seventies. The teacher contextualizes the method of teaching for the group being taught. We need to do the same for the people to whom we have been sent to "cross over and help."

We are to contend on the one hand; we must contextualize on the other. If we're going to live out a biblically faithful church, we need to do what the Bible says, and it says we have to get into the context in a way that the gospel can be proclaimed *and* understood. Paul's letters often dealt with contextualization issues: Is it all right to eat meat offered to idols? Should the Gentiles be circumcised? Does freedom allow us to have an immoral brother in our midst? Contextualization will be a weekly issue if we seek to reach the community with a relevant witness.

After all, these are our friends that we hope to reach with the gospel. They are our fellow church members in need of being cared for because of the gospel. So much as it depends on us, we should never flinch in the face of speaking with confidence about the truth presented in Christ and living out the implications of His salvation in our lives.

Living This Out

Imagine a church filled with people saying:

- "Don't worry about my preferences. Let's do what it takes to reach this community."

- "Increase giving to missions? Sure, we can cover social events from our own pockets."

- "Well, the community is Hispanic now. Should our staff reflect that?"

Remember Sonny, whom we introduced in the fourth chapter? After he had been at his new church for a short time, Philip spoke with him. Sonny excitedly explained how his storefront church had bought a piece of property and would break ground early the following year. He went on to tell Philip that he was pressing the members of his church to construct the largest building they could that would help the community. Sonny had actually done a little demographic study of the area where the property had been bought, only to find out the population was nothing like those in his church. The community was young and his church was old. The community was full of active families. His church was older people who enjoyed potluck dinners. So, as is true to his demeanor, he was the spark in the room, but this time it was to contextualize the ministry to a new location. He said, "After all, the church is not here for them. It is here for the people who aren't here yet." Sounds like he got the Macedonian call.

Points for Personal Reflection and Group Discussion

1. Has there been a time in your life when you felt called to "cross over and help" someone or a group of people? Describe it.

2. How can a church become more active in going into the community rather than staying on the church property?

3. Think about a mission trip or project you have participated in and describe what you had to "give up" for a short time.

4. What "close-quarter combat" ministries are you involved in currently? Which ones should you engage in?

5. Read Luke 4:18–19. Who in your community is in need of the service you as a believer, your group, or your church can provide?

6. Are there specific countries or people groups you are drawn to help? How could you share this burden with your pastor and church leadership to begin the work of the gospel among a new people?

have so domesticated
was designed to be—
of Christ's missio
must seek fo

Chapter 9

JOINED BY LOVE

LOVING THE CHURCH AND BEING LOVED IN CHURCH

M y wife and I were standing in the front of the church shortly after I'd finished speaking, and we were greeting people who came up to chat. After saying good-bye to a couple, I turned to shake hands with a man who'd been anxiously waiting for his turn.

He told me that he'd read every one of my books, heard me speak at several conferences, and considered me a mentor to him in his Christian walk.

Then he told me he had introduced quite a few of his friends, including several pastors, to my work, and they'd all traveled from around the country to hear me speak that particular day. I began thinking, *Wow! I really like this guy.*

But then, my *admirer* began to verbally attack my *wife*—who was standing right beside me! He said that he thinks my wife, who has been the love of my life and a partner in ministry for 25 years, is a drain on my ability to influence others. He said she's obsolete, that the "old girl is a bit faded."

I was in shock. I was upset and about to act accordingly. Then, I wondered, *What would Jesus do?* Honestly, I think Jesus would have been ticked—like any normal husband would be if his wife were attacked. I mean, you don't mess with a man's wife, and Jesus' "wife" is the church—we are the Bride of Christ.

Loving the Bride of Christ

OK, the story is not real. I made up something similar for an article I wrote. But the reality is not made up: Professing believers say and do disrespectful things about the Bride of Christ—the church. And what they say often is far more serious. You can't say you love Jesus and abuse His wife.

Unfortunately, there is a wind blowing across western Evangelicalism today that has caused churches to drift into dangerous waters. At LifeWay Research, we were surprised that the most common reasons young adults give for dropping out of church have to do with lifestyle decisions.[1] The top ten reasons young adults gave for dropping out of church:

- Simply wanted a break from church.
- Church members seemed judgmental or hypocritical.

- Moved to college and stopped attending church.
- Work responsibilities prevented me from attending.
- Moved too far away from the church to continue attending
- Became too busy, though still wanted to attend.
- Didn't feel connected to the people in my church.
- Disagreed with the church's stance on political/social issues.
- Chose to spend more time with friends outside the church.
- Was only going to church to please others.

In other words, they got too busy, moved too far away, or made some other life change. And, in their new list of priorities, the church fell toward the bottom of the list.

How can anyone give even a cursory read to the New Testament and miss the supreme importance given to the church by the One who is most Supreme? Paul says we *"were once alienated and hostile in [mind] because of [our] evil actions. But now He has reconciled [us] by His physical body through His death, to present [us] holy, faultless, and blameless before Him"* (Colossians 1:21–22). Paul goes on to say he rejoices in his sufferings because his suffering is *"completing in [his] flesh what is lacking in Christ's afflictions for His body, that is, the church"* (Colossians 1:24).

Created by God, not human beings

Paul was willing to take a beating for the church because Jesus submitted to a brutal murder *"to make her [the church] holy, cleansing her in the washing of water by the word. He did this to present the church to Himself in splendor, without spot or wrinkle or anything like that, but holy and blameless"* (Ephesians 5:26–27).

Seems fewer people are willing to take the church seriously, let alone take a beating for her. Just in these two key passages, Paul teaches that Jesus—who clearly founded the church (Matthew 16:18)—suffered the physical brutality of God's righteous retribution against our spiritual rebellion. Jesus did this in order to present an intentionally gathered people—His church—into His presence through His holiness.

In *Serious Times*, author James Emery White writes, "Christ followers are notorious for being dismissive of the church, as if it were a disposable institution created by human beings."[2]

It is easy to see that many churches are not fulfilling God's mission. And, by doing so, many have considered it unnecessary. Like a ship being pulled off course, our churches are drifting. So what are we to do? We need to, once again, fall in love with the church.

The church is important to the work of God. Paul says the multifaceted wisdom of God may now be made known *through the church*. What's included in that multifaceted wisdom? *"The incalculable riches of the Messiah, and [the shedding of] light for all about the administration of the mystery hidden for ages in God who created all things"* (Ephesians 3:8–9).

The remedy for drifting Christianity

Another answer: Don't panic! The church belongs to Jesus and He will protect His Bride! In North America, we may see many believers dismissing the church. However, in the rest of the world, people are still dying for her. There are still people in North America who have a high view of Christ's Bride and seek to serve her with their lives. We just need to know she is not in danger of disappearing.

It is ironic that the very remedy for our sinking, drifting Christianity is found in the very institution many are weakening, marginalizing, and walking away from. We have the institution through which the risen Christ plans to capture the hearts of rebellious men, yet we scamper here and there after wispy spiritual experiences. Amazing!

White continues in *Serious Times*:

"We do not live and breathe in a neutral environment but in the midst of a hostile conflict, and we are behind enemy lines. The god of this world has been named, and he is ensconced firmly on his throne. There is only one domain beyond his control that stands in the way of total dominion: the body of Christ. As a result, the church is under constant assault, for it stands alone against the night. It demands constant reinforcement and steadfast commitment. The church is not simply the vanguard of kingdom advance; it is the entire assault force. According to Jesus' words, the church is not only to take a stand against evil but also to stage a frontal attack."[3]

The church is central to God's plan

Now, let me say that the church is not the *center* of God's plan—Jesus is. But the church is *central* to God's plan.

Jesus taught that the church is in a position of great importance. It doesn't matter if a congregation meets in a cathedral or a coffee shop; it is still the church, and the church matters. If you claim to be a disciple of Jesus, then it stands to reason you're going to love His Bride. Don't be guilty of going to great lengths to show love for Christ while ignoring, marginalizing, or attacking the Bride. We can't love Jesus and hate His wife. Loving the church—that is, loving one another in the church—is the mark of a Christian.

For the members of the church, loving one another should be natural. But we are altogether too frail in our humanity, and our flesh gets in the way of that imperative. Jesus plainly spells out how the church is to be identified: *"I give you a new command: Love one another. Just as I have loved you, you must also love one another. By this all people will know that you are My disciples, if you have love for one another"* (John 13:34–35). The very marker of the church to the watching world is an obvious love for one another inside the church.

One of the ways we can explore how to express love in the church is the New Testament imagery regarding the church. From Christ's words in the Gospels to the final revelation given to John, God has used numerous metaphors to picture the church, the components of which allow us to learn more about the love we are to have for one another within the church.

The Household of God

The portrait of those living in a household provides one of the most intimate scenes of love. If not intimate, then at least it's the place where we fight best with those we love most deeply!

The role of family among Christ's followers was illustrated at Christ's crucifixion when He gave His mother into the care of John by redefining their relationship as mother and son (John 19:26–27). Paul further illuminated it by perceiving Timothy as his son in the ministry. He even wrote, *"But if I should be delayed, I have written so that you will know how people ought to act in God's household, which is the church of the living God, the pillar and foundation of the truth"* (1 Timothy 3:15). Paul described the church as "God's household" (Ephesians 2:19) and the "household of faith" (Galatians 6:10). Peter's writing also alludes to this image as he described the church as the "brotherhood" (1 Peter 2:17), meaning a Christian community of brothers and sisters.

Love in the church shines forth in this image of a family. In a family, loving one another is a necessity. After all, what is a family if it's devoid of love? And what is the church if its members lose their love for one another?

Another aspect to the family image of the church is its relation to the Father. We are told to cry out to the Father with the Hebrew term *Abba* (Galatians 4:6). It's a word still heard in the Middle East today. There are some who have overestimated the sentimentality of the word by saying it is the same as the English word *Daddy*.

Now, I love it when my children look at me with their big puppy-dog eyes and say "Daddy" in a voice that would melt the hardest of hearts. And we often speak to God as a humble child, but there is much more to the title Abba than the emotions between a daddy and his babies. The term has much more to do with intimacy than infancy. In fact, the Mishna (Jewish religious law) contains texts that indicate Abba was a designation grown children used to claim their inheritance from a deceased father.[4] The term speaks of a family relationship where care is taken of the children.

The Old Testament did not provide context for our modern practice of adoption. However, "something very like adoption is implied in Yahweh's relation to Israel, his 'firstborn son' (Exodus 4:22; Hosea 11:1)." Roman emperors in the first and second centuries A.D. began the practice of adopting men not related to them by blood "with the intention that they should succeed them in the principate."[5]

Knowing this, we see the household image sets the stage for both our intimate relation to the Father and the continuation of His sovereign work on earth as we are heirs to His kingdom. This helps us understand the divine mission within the relationships we have with one another as a family. John Stott reminds us, "Sonship implies responsibility."[6] As modern believers delve into what it means to be members of God's household, the responsibility to fulfill the Father's desires becomes clear.

We should not just love our new siblings in Christ, but we also should find ways for others to hear the news about our adopting Father. Many churches have a mission statement that reads something like: "Leading people to become fully devoted followers of Jesus."

As fascinating as it is for us to consider the relationship between adopted child and parent, the relationship between adopted siblings is equally interesting. The Father's desire is to show loving benevolence. Toward the members of God's household, we should exhibit a similar love, especially when they are new to the family. His adopting love is one we can imitate as new believers are added to the family of faith.

Not all of us were readily welcomed into the church. Perhaps due to previous sin or a bad reputation, some believers may have been either standoffish or condescending to you. But now that we clearly see how kind the Father's welcome is to new children in the faith, we should follow His example. Rather than obsess over a person's preconversion reputation, we should welcome that person as a new creation in Christ. As children (and sometimes adults), brothers and sisters have a nasty habit of fighting with one another. In the church, we should set aside childlike behavior and care for one another in the complete manner offered to us, and expected by, the Father.

The love of a family is certainly an excellent picture of the overall function of the church. Familial love is shown through caring for the less fortunate of a community (whether widows in the ancient world or AIDS patients in today's era), in the biblical function of fellowship, and in the missionary thrust of the church. The love that originates in Christ and is expressed through

128

His sacrificial death must be communicated through the service of believers toward one another. We are called to love.

One thing about church that affects people is the fact that family members fight. Somewhere, years ago, I heard an old preacher say, "The church would be all right if it weren't for all the people." The truth is, we are a dysfunctional family as long as we are still on this earth. Most of the dysfunction comes as family members assert their rights and want their preferences, rather than keeping their eyes on the field that is "ready for harvest" (John 4:35).

The Body of Christ

The "body of Christ" is one of the leading images in Paul's writings in the New Testament. Significant references to this symbol for the church can be found in Romans, 1 Corinthians, Ephesians, and Colossians. The metaphor of the body conveys characteristics of interdependence and activity in a body that would have been as apparent to the original readers as they are to us now.

Activity is vital to the life of the church. "Christ directs, controls, and energizes the members (albeit through the 'ligaments' of Ephesians 4:16) so that they may serve his purpose in the world."[7] This activity is easily seen as Paul discusses, in Ephesians 4:4–13, the gifts that are placed within the body. The specific work is shown in verses 12–13 as Paul calls the members of the body to use their gifts *"for the training of the saints in the work of ministry, to build up the body of Christ, until we all reach unity in the faith and in the knowledge of God's Son, growing into a mature man with a stature measured by Christ's fullness."*

The church exists, among other things, to assist in maturing the fellowship and increasing the numbers of those being saved. As Christ's body, we are His agent of care in the world. So often this is applied exclusively to those outside the faith who we are trying to bring to salvation. With Paul's teaching to the Ephesians, we see that our loving service is to result in the church attaining unity, maturity, and fullness in Christ.

So many people want to feel the arms of God hugging them and experience the hands of God serving them. They can—in our actions.

We are the arms and hands of God that reach out to a hurt and dying world, not focused on self-absorption that makes the church lazy or fighting with each other. Our relationship with Christ should compel the body to reach out to those who are not yet a part of the body. His love for them should be evident in us.

When we decide a "lesser" member of the church isn't really needed in the ministry, we should think seriously about what God has said. From God's vantage point, all the parts to the body He is assembling are vital to His work (1 Corinthians 12:14–26). If the people I attend church with are so vital to God, then our proper response to them is one of love and service. To those in our congregations, we should be as a squire to a knight: Whatever they need for war on behalf of the King, we ensure they are resourced and fit for battle.

It is evident in the common work of the church that great fellowship and intimacy are born from working toward a common goal. This should be more evident in the body of Christ than anywhere else. Our churches should take the time needed to emphasize our unity of purpose and heart over and against our disparities.

An Old Testament illustration of this unity is found in Nehemiah 3. An unusual thing happened along the way as Nehemiah led the people to God's agenda of rebuilding the wall around Jerusalem. Everyone combined their effort to build a wall and repair the gates, regardless of their vocational skills. Among the amateur masons and carpenters are priests, goldsmiths, perfume makers, daughters, rulers, Levites/song leaders, temple servants, guards, and merchants. Everyone set aside what they were comfortable doing on a daily basis in order to join God's people in working toward a common goal. For the body of Christ, there comes a time when, no matter what your skill set, there is only one thing that must be done. Nothing brings a church together like a great task or a great crisis!

The application to unity is clear. Any power brokering or dissension in the local body will virtually eliminate its usefulness to the kingdom's work. Conversely, as a church body works in the loving unity of the Trinity, the diversity of gifts that is available under the Spirit's direction can be useful for any ministry focused on God's glory.

Dilbert comic strips and the sitcom *The Office* are popular for a reason: They are a comedic but fairly accurate portrayal of the offices we work in every day. Programs such as *Desperate Housewives* strike a chord with many because the strained relationships seem to mirror their own lives (even if the situations are surreal). So there is no doubt the world will take notice of a group of varied individuals who work in harmony for the same mission. Since making disciples takes a varied approach, each believer and church must continue to look toward the Head for their specific roles so we will love one another properly and witness effectively.

The Flock of God

Perhaps one of the most adored images of the church is that of the shepherd and his flock. This image has evangelized the lost, comforted the distressed, and given direction to the pilgrim for centuries. It finds its greatest description in John 10 but is referred to in Matthew, Acts, and 1 Peter as well.

One fact seems undeniable in all the images observed in this chapter: The Lord of the church is great in power and love. The flock image is no different. Jesus as the Great Shepherd of the church is shown to be the sincere and heroic shepherd ready to lay down his life for the sheep. Jesus claims to be the only keeper of access to security and life eternal. In contrast, the Pharisees and the religious leaders of the day are revealed to be thieves who would steal from the sheepfold. Ultimately, the flock finds no safety except in Jesus Christ (John 10:11–13).

We watch many churches work out of fear—fear of closing their doors, fear of not making budget, fear of a changing culture creeping to its doors. As Christ's flock, what or whom should we fear? With Jesus as the Good Shepherd, fear is unnecessary.

As we lead our churches to evangelize and grow, the shepherd's seeking attitude must be paramount in the mind of today's believers. It is often more comfortable and easier to serve as the chaplain for a holy huddle of believers who will stroke one's ego. This applies to pastors, Bible study leaders, youth ministry workers, and greeters at the door. However, the example of Christ compels the church to get out and engage in searching the countryside for the lost sheep.

The application of this message can come at a great price to a local congregation. After all, bringing a formerly lost sheep back home can create stress in a flock. The love of God lived through the church should override any tension brought when a wayward believer is reclaimed or a new one is redeemed. Our joy should be in finding the one who has gone missing from the company of the gospel.

This leads to the image of nurturing God's flock. The shepherd should provide sustenance to the flock. Psalm 23 serves as a precursor of the relationship God has with His people in the New Covenant. In that passage, sheep are led to green pastures and calm waters to receive nourishment. As John 10:4 says, the sheep know the shepherd's voice; Christ is known intimately in a personal relationship with members of the church. John Calvin wrote that there is a spirit of discernment among the flock "by which the elect discriminate between the truth of God and men's false inventions."[8] It is as though all of our children are playing at the park. When a child falls, though there is the clamor of other voices, a mom clearly hears the cry of her child. We should be so attuned to our Shepherd's voice.

As the church grows, it does so not only in number but also in maturity. Discipleship of the flock occurs by the leadership of Christ as the Great Shepherd and human undershepherds. Peter called the elders of the early church to be examples in life and doctrine to the flock of God (1 Peter 5:1–4). God is seeking the lost sheep both for personal growth and the expansion of His kingdom. This growth can most easily occur in an environment of caring love for one another.

The Bride of Christ

The final image for us to consider is the Bride of Christ. God established the institution of marriage for many reasons. But among them all, its greatest is to serve as a picture of the relationship between Christ and the church. As with any marriage, there is to be love, faithfulness, and commitment between bride and groom. So it is with Christ and the church. The New Testament is replete with calls for devotion toward Christ as He is always faithful toward the church (2 Timothy 2:11–13; Romans 3:3–4). The image of the bride is a heavenly portrait we cannot help but be drawn toward.

First, there is a call for purity on the part of the bride or the church. Paul told the Corinthian believers, *"For I am jealous over you with a godly jealousy, because I have promised you in marriage to one husband—to present a pure virgin to Christ"* (2 Corinthians 11:2). It is well established that Christ, as the bridegroom, is without sin. So the call for fidelity lies with believers. The church is to love Christ in such great manner that we would be presented to Him as a virgin upon His arrival.

Unlike human grooms, Christ has the power to ensure a pure bride. Paul wrote in Ephesians 5:26–27 that Christ would make the church *"holy, cleansing her with the washing of water by the word. He did this to present the church to Himself in splendor, without spot or wrinkle or anything like that, but holy and blameless."* It is the will of God that the church be holy. Aiding one another in purity should come naturally to us. Just as bridesmaids help the bride look perfect on her wedding day, so should we look out for one another as we await the Bridegroom. *"Let us be glad, rejoice, and give Him glory, because the marriage of the Lamb has come, and His wife has prepared herself. She was given fine linen to wear, bright and pure. For the fine linen represents the righteous acts of the saints"* (Revelation 19:7–8). This portrait of the eternal residence the church will have with Christ should inspire us whenever we gather in worship.

In marriage, commitment naturally results in protectiveness. Throughout his ministry, Paul worked to aid the church in remaining a faithful virgin awaiting the consummation of her commitment to Christ. It's a blessing to stand as the bride who awaits a jealous and adoring groom.

Philip and Angie were married in the sanctuary of First Baptist Church of Jonesboro, Georgia, in 1994. He explains: "I can still remember the surge of adrenaline and the palpitations of my heart in the moments before she entered the room. Everyone else faded into oblivion when the doors opened and there she stood; that was the most breathtaking moment. She didn't walk down the aisle; she glided down the aisle. Her white gown, beautiful smile, and expectant heart were all a foretaste of the beauty of marriage.

"By God's blessings, I was called to serve on staff of the same church six years later. One of my Sunday morning duties entailed standing at the front of the sanctuary during the invitation following the sermon. I saw hundreds of people walk the aisle to have a counselor lead them to Christ, join the church, or seek prayer. But one specific thought always lingered in my mind: my wedding day. For I had the unusual honor of standing in the same spot each Sunday where I had stood when Angie walked the aisle to meet me as her groom."

Philip's experience reminded him just how sacred the covenant of marriage truly is. The groom and bride commit themselves to one another in such a way that they are now one. The implications for the church is that *you cannot love Jesus and deny love to His Bride.* God gives a place of esteem to the Bride that is unlike any other in creation. Too many in the believing community are growing weary of the Bride due to her imperfections on a local level or denominational wrangling at a national level.

We are not given that option with Christ. After all, we aren't presented that option with other humans. If you don't like my wife, then I don't suppose we will get along at any level. I will not stand for her to be disrespected. If a groom's love for his bride is even the slightest indication of what Christ has for the church, then all believers should feel compelled to love the church (i.e., their fellow believers). As the church is faithful to Christ, each of us should maintain a faithful relationship with His wife. A betrayal of devotion to Yahweh's Bride will certainly spell disaster for any believer.

What is your church like? Do you like the people who attend worship and Bible study with you? You might even be considering changing pews just to get away from somebody else.

Now is the time to renew our love for the church. She isn't perfect yet, but neither are we. Love the people of the church, the leaders of the church, and the work of Christ through the church as we work together for the gospel of hope and love.

We cannot love a lost and dying world if we cannot love God's redeemed!

Evident love

A full accounting of love within the confines of the church is a vast undertaking. The images presented are only a few Scripture lists for the people of God. No matter which one might be our favorite, taking the time to study these images will increase our level of love in two ways. First, our appreciation for the work of Christ will increase. Secondly, we will learn why it's critical that every believer be involved in the church.

As I mentioned earlier, Philip and I served during the interim time at a church in Nashville. Philip has watched as the church seems to have gone through several phases defined by some interesting questions. He describes it this way:

"When we arrived, the church seemed to be asking a painful question: 'Can we survive?' Having endured pain, controversy, and decline, it seemed an appropriate question. God—as always—was gracious, and we watched the church family come alive and begin to ask a new question. After the devastating flood that left so many families in pain in our city, the church began to reach out and minister in new ways. Their new question was: 'How can we help?'

"Eventually, the church called a permanent pastor, and we made a quiet exit. Ed went on to plant a new church. However, the new pastor asked me to come back and serve on the staff with him as one of the teaching pastors. Now, the church rediscovered its mission, renamed the congregation to The Fellowship, and found a great deal of courage in ministry. I'm happy to say that we have a new question that defines us: 'How can we transform our city and the world with the gospel?' It is a testimony to what happens when the church lives for the mission of Christ."

Points for Personal Reflection and Group Discussion

1. When you think about church, what image comes to mind: a family that gets along well or one that argues often? How have your experiences in church colored this thinking?

2. How does the image of a household change your understanding of the relationships within a church?

3. Describe the difference it makes that God has adopted you into His family.

4. Read 1 Corinthians 12:12–26. How can this image help to remove the sins of pride and favoritism from the church?

5. Discuss how your church can continually keep Christ in His proper place, as the Head of the body.

6. In Nehemiah 3, everyone set aside their skill set in order to work on the most important task of the day. What is the one thing your church should rally around?

7. First Corinthians 3:9 describes us as *"God's coworkers."* How does that description affect your attitude in doing missional ministry?

8. Read Ephesians 5:26–27. What must occur next in your life or in the lives of those in your study group/church in order to be the pure Bride of Christ?

Part III
Formed by Love:
Believers and the World

Chapter 10

OBEDIENT LOVE

INTERSECTION OF TWO IDEALS

Our little house in Levittown had a tree in the backyard. I spent a lot of time around that tree, climbing it, carving things in it, and just generally defiling it.

One November, the trees lost their leaves in a way that seemed, well, sudden. And a big pile of leaves in the front yard was an opportunity for only one thing—a fort.

Building a leaf fort requires a rake, some muscle, and a little shaping. In a little while, we had built a great one. It was (as I remember it) five feet high and eight feet wide. We built a little turret into it, so we could see the Watsons' house (one fenced yard over). Then, with the apples that fell from a nearby tree, we could throw apple "grenades" into their pool and, with a good shot, onto their heads.

Needless to say, this was soon the talk of the neighborhood. All the other kids wanted "in." Now that didn't usually happen to us, so we relished the moment. We started making random rules: *If* you want in, *then* you have to do this. And there were a *lot* of if/then rules.

First, if you wanted to be part of the leaf fort war, you had to bring apples (most of ours were in the Watsons' pool). Second, if you wanted to be in our leaf fort club, then you had to promise to always be on our side in future neighborhood battles. Third, if you wanted in, you had to promise to be our best friends forever. Boys and girls kept coming—and kept making promises they never intended to keep.

These kinds of if/then statements are less common in the Scriptures. God reached out to us in spite of the fact that we were still sinners. But there is one if/then that stands out above the others: *"If you love Me, [then] you will keep My commands"* (John 14:15). It's not a condition that's required to be in or receive God's grace, but it is a result of genuine love in relationship with God.

Love and Obedience

Love and obedience intersect. Humanity has fought to separate the ideas of obedience and love. Not consciously, but we have fought nonetheless. The human-centered view of love is not one bowing to another but all others bowing to me. From the earth, love is *self-serving*. From heaven's view, it is *obeying*. A simple look toward Gethsemane and Calvary makes it clear.

Obedience and love intermingle throughout the Scriptures. When asked as to the greatest command, Jesus said it is to love God with our whole being (Matthew 22:37). We now commonly refer to this statement by Jesus as the Great Commandment, an appropriate companion to the Great Commission. The command to love this way is contrary to human intuition. We prefer coming to love by our own standards and because of our own reasons. When *ordered* to love, we say it isn't love at all.

We can once again take marriage as an example for why we love. I am compelled to love my wife because she extended her life to me. Without that gracious move on her part, I still would be single. In an infinitely greater act, God loves me first so I would know to reciprocate (1 John 4:19). The Scriptures paint a picture of a provoked love on account of God's initiative.

John is the apostle most identified with the ideal of love. He's even known by biblical scholars as the beloved disciple. It's appropriate that in the Gospels he alone is given the privilege of writing these words of Jesus: *"If you love Me, you will keep My commands"* (John 14:15). In fact, the word *love* is used 79 times throughout John's New Testament writings (39 in his Gospel, 33 in his three epistles, and 7 times in the Revelation). The other three Gospels by Matthew, Mark, and Luke use the word a combined total of 29 times. Obviously, the Lord desires to teach us something from John's writings.

John personally loved Christ deeply. He participated in Jesus' inner circle, along with Peter and James. Of the apostles, John alone survived martyrdom. He lived to an old age and he died in exile on the island of Patmos—after receiving the apocalyptic vision of God's conclusion to human history. He was inspired to write about love properly placed on God and horribly misplaced on sin. John understood the compulsion of love in the face of deity.

In his first letter to the early church, John seeks to correct doctrinal errors and to heal a potential split in the church. In doing so, much of his focus is on having the proper love for God. Perhaps much of the division in our own churches and denominations would fade into history if we could, as John taught, connect to an obedient love for Christ. Obedience to Christ's mission will bring about love for the body of Christ and for the work assigned to us.

"This is how we are sure that we have come to know Him: by keeping His commands" (1 John 2:3). The idea of knowing God is one the whole world is seeking, but we have the same issue our ancestors did in Genesis 11—we think too highly of ourselves. In that passage, the people were ready to replace obeying God with their own self-aggrandizement. Trading their relationship with God with self-promotion was, at best, foolish. At worse, it was disastrous. But pride in our own thinking will never lead us deeper into God's mission for His people.

A love that's personal

The human compulsion is to discover *things*. Why else would we send rocket ships to the moon, send submarines to the depths of the oceans, and watch wildlife teams wrestle pythons and crocodiles on television? We want to know more, but mere knowledge isn't enough. Humans desire a personal experience. This is perfectly illustrated in the evolution of video games.

Philip's first video game was a Sears console with Pong, Video Pinball, and Breakout—a clunky brown box with three buttons and a dial. The screen offered only block-like action, but it was state of the art at the time. As video games progressed, characters were introduced—heroes like Pac-Man saving Mrs. Pac-Man, and the Super Mario Brothers searching for Princess Peach, and Link saving Princess Zelda.

But then came what seemed to be an ultimate moment for gamers—*Tron*. It was a movie centered on the idea of a computer hacker being abducted into the world of a video game. *Tron* was a milestone. From that point on, video games became more about personalities and personal experiences than moving blocks around a screen.

Today, "first-person" is the standard for high-end video games. Whether driving a race car or interacting with other characters, humans want an experience, even in the cyberworld. The technology has pushed ever further than just seeing the game from a character's perspective. Now, through game systems like Wii and Kinect, by use of motion sensors, your body is the game controller. We've gone from buttons and knobs on a clunky box to making our game characters mimic our physical movement in the real world.

The Apostle John says it's possible to personally experience God's love, but the path to that experience is down the road of obedience. In other words, seeking more *knowledge* of God is not the way to experience God's love. Instead, it's a by-product of our obedience to God and a result of God initiating an intimate relationship with us.

Yet we tend to think the opposite—that knowledge brings about obedience. But the accumulation of knowledge is a poor definition for discipleship or active participation in God's mission. Knowledge without love is meaningless; what matters is how it is used. It's just like fire. Fire is neither good nor bad; how it is used is what makes the difference. In a fireplace, a blaze can warm a house, a soul, or a romantic relationship. Move the fire into the middle of the living room, and it produces nothing but negative results.

God's commands reflect His love

We must seek obedience first! From that obedience comes the knowledge of how to be more obedient and how to love more deeply. Obedience provides the proper place for knowledge to reside.

Soldiers in the midst of a firefight with the enemy have a limited view of the battlefield. Their victory and survival relies on their commanding officers, who have access to satellites, maps, scouts, and the battle plan. Soldiers must trust and obey the orders of their commanders, who see the entire battlefield. We share that same situation. It is critical for our love to be rightly placed on God. We must obey Him so we will know Him and participate with Christ in victory.

Like a commanding general, God has the right to expect our obedience. Our flesh, however, tells us to rebel against any rule—even the rules that are for our own good. Much of this attitude is the perception that rules are "hard." Rules cramp our style and get in the way of a good time. Later in his letter, John addresses this attitude:

For this is what love for God is: to keep His commands. Now His commands are not a burden, because whatever has been born of God conquers the world. This is the victory that has conquered the world: our faith. And who is the one who conquers the world but the one who believes that Jesus is the Son of God?

—1 JOHN 5:3–5

We too often look at the idea of spiritual obedience like a teenager looks at the rules set out by a parent. Sighing with displeasure, our teenagers go about the oppressive work of cleaning their rooms (Oh, the horror!), taking out the trash (I can't stand it!), or showering on a regular basis (It's just too much!). But none of these requirements are a great burden. Ultimately, they are for the good of the family—which includes the teenager. As the parent, you know that the "rules" are for their own good and are in no way oppressive.

It's only by obedience that we gain enough relief from the world to have knowledge of God. Children may see rules as overbearing, but for the believer, the commands of God are a delight. Through their keeping, we can be drawn closer to God and His victory over the world. Burdens lower a soul; God's commands raise it.

Obedience completes our love

In the climactic moment of the film, *Jerry McGuire,* Tom Cruise says to Renée Zellweger, "You complete me." It's the moment of the movie everyone was waiting for—a zenith experience where two souls connect and life makes sense. Many are searching for that one thing that will bring a sense of completion to life.

The entrepreneur finds meaning in the business deal. Artists find it in producing something beautiful in clay, music, or another medium. Parents often find it in their children. But all of these pursuits are temporary. Those who love Christ supremely seek to find meaning in God's glory and fame, which is forever.

I'm not an artist, but like you I have tried my hand at doodling on paper. When we see a true artist paint with effortless strokes of the brush, it seems as if anyone can do it. So what's missing that causes my doodles to look—well, like doodles? I don't know the rules of art. True masters of the arts naturally know and follow the rules. They have acclimated their eyes to see how light falls in the scene and the proportion of one object to another in the two-dimensional world of the canvas. I, however, do not know the rules. I can only generate squiggles on a napkin.

First John 2:5 taught the early church and teaches us: *"But whoever keeps His word, truly in him the love of God is perfected. This is how we know we are in Him."* To complete the portrait of my love for God, obedience is the requirement, and my obedience ultimately shows who I can be for Him.

Later in John's first letter, he reiterates the idea: *"No one has ever seen God. If we love one another, God remains in us and His love is perfected in us"* (1 John 4:12). The context of the passage is relationships within the church. The completing work of God's love in our lives finds no border. It is pervasive in its influence upon us. As the life of Christ revolutionizes our lives, God's love cycles us to love others so His presence can have more power over us. His kingdom is present because we are obedient to His ruling power.

God's love spans the gap

There are times when we must "force" ourselves to be nice. Perhaps you work with someone who is well-meaning but difficult to take. A little gruff on Mondays and impatient on Fridays, but you coerce a pleasant attitude out of yourself. The answer is to stop simply trying to be nice and *love*. Work for that person's best interests. The second half of the Great Commandment is: *"Love your neighbor as yourself"* (Matthew 22:39). As we love, God's loving presence shown through us will make up the difference because mere emotions will always fail. He will mature our character so that participating in His mission of love and redemption becomes our default mode of living.

One of the most effective tools to move us from "nice" to "love" is prayer.

We must learn to pray that our attitudes toward a person or a situation will change. We also need to pray that God will work for the good of that person. Once we begin to pray in that manner, we can't help but love.

Obedience proves our love

Can we prove love? There isn't a mathematical equation for it. The scientific method doesn't apply to it. Not even the metric system has a measurement for it! Yet God tells us how love can be verified—by its expression in living.

As I said, God's love expressed in us should not find a border in our life. He has a sweeping effect upon us. As He establishes His love within us, others will experience it. John states it this way: *"This is how we know that we love God's children when we love God and obey His commands"* (1 John 5:2). The extent to which we love others is a test to undergo for believers. If found wanting in the arena of love, then participating in God's mission is relatively unlikely on our part.

God's demonstration of love toward His children is powerful. He brings comfort to the mourning through those who have mourned. He loves His Bride—the church—through men and women who have pledged their love to one another at the altar. He matures His children by spiritual parents who dedicate their lives to raising infant believers. The church knows the love of God because the love of God is evident in the church.

The world also witnesses the love of God through our love for one another. To be missional, we have to love the children of God. *"By this all people will know that you are My disciples, if you have love for one another"* (John 13:35). The whole world should be able to identify the believers among them. The church, on mission, should be constantly proving the reality of God's love by the way we care, comfort, and enjoy one another.

The heart of the missional Christian is buoyed by love. The action of the missional Christian is directed by obedience. Obedience, for all its worth, comes with some difficulty. When we are first saved, obeying Christ is exciting. Nothing else matters at the moment. Passing from darkness to light often outshines the tempter's snare and the lust of the flesh.

However, the Wet Blanket Committee seems invariably to get around to all new believers. They are the ones who try to settle down the new believer. These men and women come along with the commendable desire for young believers to not burn themselves out too soon. Fearfully, all of their intentions are likely born from a loss of zeal in their own lives. The real effect of their "encouragement" to new believers is to diminish a person's love and obedience toward Christ. Rather than asking new believers to settle down or settle in, we should learn from their excitement to love and obey. The church should rally around their unbridled passion to follow God's will and mission.

I say, let the new believers loose on the world. They were changed by the gospel of love and glory. Tell them to obey the Lord who authored their release. Better yet, help them live under His beautiful commands, which are light and life to the soul.

Our missional endeavor ought to involve every new Christian in our sphere of influence, both young and old. Set the children as greeters at the door. Take your daughter who was just converted to visit her friend's family that is outside of Christ and let her watch as you tell them of Christ's enduring love. Team up with an adult who was just converted to minister in the community and find ways to serve cups of cold water in the name of Jesus. As we love the church as Christ loves the church, obedience to His commands will purify our passions and lead us to a greater ministry of disciple making.

Points for Personal Reflection and Group Discussion

1. Where do people generally turn for a sense of fulfillment in their lives?

2. How does the gospel change your perspective on obeying God's principles in scripture?

3. How are obedience to God's mission and love related to one another?

4. How can your life begin giving more evidence of God's love in the church? In your family? At work? In the world?

5. Discuss the effects if our knowledge of Scripture outpaces our love for God.

6. What principles of the Scriptures have you learned that are difficult to obey? Why do you find yourself rebelling against these particular truths?

7. If obedience is the measure of our love for God, list the practical ways in which you could begin to see love growing in your life.

8. How can your church begin to unleash the lives of new believers who are children?

9. What can your group do to aid the growth of a new believer who is an adult?

Chapter 11

GUIDED BY LOVE

SEEKING TO DO THE WILL OF THE FATHER

Having been reared Catholic, I knew a lot about trying harder. We attended St. Bernard's Catholic Church, at least on Christmas and Easter. The church building was a former aircraft hanger servicing Mitchel Field, redone into a church when the potato farms of Nassau County became Levittown, the world's most famous tract housing.

I don't remember hearing much about how the love of God worked in our lives, but we did learn a lot about what we should *do*—and I carried that false understanding of the faith for a while, even after I became a Christian. I wrote a reflection of my 30th spiritual birthday at my blog (www.edstetzer.com), excerpted here.

I committed my life to Christ 30 years ago today. . . . It was at a youth camp in Central Florida. While the band played "Turn Your Eyes upon Jesus," I did. And I threw my life and hopes "upon Jesus" too. A few things surprised me on the journey.

I thought I would have been more holy by now—that I would have overcome the flesh, be more consistent in my spiritual walk, and just be a better Christian. But, I have learned that Paul was right in that "the very things I want to do I just don't do" (see Romans 7:15). Keith Green used to sing a song based on Romans 7 that I listened to as a new believer ("I Want to Be More Like Jesus")—I would passionately sing the part "Lord it seems so sad, why am I so bad, when in my heart I only want to be like you." As I grew in understanding the Scriptures, I learned that does not change until I am set free from the "body of this death" (Romans 7:24 KJV).

Although I shouldn't be, I am surprised at how many believers I know are not "more holy by now." A few years after becoming a Christian, I began to see that many of my early Christian heroes had clay feet. And, for that matter, so many of the Christian leaders I fellowship with today are insecure, selfish, and driven by agendas other than the Cross—like I am at times. I guess it should not surprise me as I read the New Testament. They had their issues too.

I am surprised at how little I understood the gospel when I became a Christian, and how that gospel would become so important later. I wish

I had known more about the Cross and the saving life of Christ. I think my Christian life would have been much less "try harder" and much more "trust Jesus."

As I grew in my faith, I discovered Christianity is not an ethical code or series of rules by which we live. No, it is something more.

But, before I get to the something more, I must confess I have found the *rule-making* version of Christianity to be relatively standard-issue practice in much of North America. It seems the natural state of religious learning is toward making, keeping, and enforcing rules. Our hearts are rule machines, always preferring the comfort of rules that tell us what to do instead of a love relationship where we know God for who He is.

Finding God and His Will

"How can I know the will of God?" is one of the questions we both love and fear. We love it because it holds the promise of a great beginning point and never-ending answers. We sometimes fear it because we are unsure of what God's will might cost us. Nevertheless, the issue of doing the will of the Father is one which saints and sages have wrestled over for centuries.

The temptation in answering the question is to set a pinpoint agenda for everyone to follow. We look for sequential orders that arrive at prescribed endings. When dealing with the unknown, we tend to make our lives as neat and nice as possible.

But God's agenda is not always tidy. It does not often fit into our step-by-step approach. At times, God calls us to unusual circumstances, directions, and destinations. Yet it only *seems* they're unusual because we're accustomed to our own dreams and ambitions. Too often, we substitute our hopes for God's plan.

Psalm 8:6–8 praises the sovereignty of God over all creation. It's a word of thanks that He's placed mankind as caretaker over animals, birds, and fish of the sea. Yet, in the midst of this thankfulness that God has given us stewardship of the earth, there's a reminder to its order:

You made him lord over the works of Your hands; You put everything under his feet: all the sheep and oxen, as well as the animals in the wild, the birds of the sky, and the fish of the sea that pass through the currents of the seas.

—PSALM 8:6–8

We should not skip the final phrase: *"and the fish of the sea that pass through the currents of the sea."* Looking into the ocean, we see creatures in random motion. But the meaning of the phrase is that God has set paths even for the fish. If that isn't random, then certainly our lives aren't random either. If there is a path for the tuna and the squid, then there is a path for you and me—even if it is an unexpected path.

Leaving behind the temptation of an easy 1-2-3 process for knowing and following God's will leads us to focus on our character. A properly developed character by the Father can easily fulfill the agenda for the missionary endeavor He sets before us. Human hearts and minds tuned to God's heart and mind will naturally hear, see, and follow God's will.

But first . . .

It's important to note here: Follow the *revealed will* of God before going after some secret plan. The Bible is God's epic telling of His glorious pursuit for us— so that we will know and follow Him. It describes how our lives bring honor to Him when we are singularly devoted to Him—bearing one another's burdens, resisting the enemy, and preparing ourselves for His triumphal, apocalyptic return.

The Bible gives His revealed will, which provides guidelines for living out His kingdom values in this rebellious world. As our character is developed properly by the Father, we can easily fulfill the agenda for the missionary endeavor He sets before us. Yet knowing we're to proclaim the gospel is easy; knowing to whom and how we're to proclaim it—*in a given moment*—seems to be a different matter. The *personalization* of God's will is what we seek.

The Apostle Paul understood the Christians in Rome were struggling with the same issue:

Do not owe anyone anything, except to love one another, for the one who loves another has fulfilled the law. The commandments: Do not commit adultery; do not murder; do not steal; do not covet; and whatever other commandment —all are summed up by this: Love your neighbor as yourself. Love does no wrong to a neighbor. Love, therefore, is the fulfillment of the law. Besides this, knowing the time, it is already the hour for you to wake up from sleep, for now our salvation is nearer than when we first believed. The night is nearly over, and the daylight is near, so let us discard the deeds of darkness and put on the armor of light. Let us walk with decency, as in the daylight: not in carousing and drunkenness; not in sexual impurity and promiscuity; not in quarreling and jealousy. But put on the Lord Jesus Christ, and make no plans to satisfy the fleshly desires.

—ROMANS 13:8–14

This passage reveals some of what we must have to follow God's agenda.

The proper debt: Love

Paul speaks about the debt of love in verse 8: *"Do not owe anyone anything, except to love one another."* Two thousand years later, we're still familiar with what it means to be in debt. I don't own a house yet. Instead, I owe a mortgage company. Many people are indebted to a finance company for a car. I am indebted to friends for always being there for me. Certainly, I am indebted to my wife for marrying me. We feel as if we are constantly paying back others.

Paul tells the early believers in Rome that the only debt we owe— *spiritually*—is that of loving one another. But we tend to replace activity as the priority: learning a new evangelistic technique, warning of impending judgment, or fulfilling a social need. Advocating a higher way, the charge is to love. This shouldn't surprise us, though. In the midst of a church culture with a hyper-focus on the "spiritual gifts," Paul pointed out in 1 Corinthians 12:31 the need to see beyond our abilities, even supernatural ones. *"And I will show you an even better way."* At the end of the passage that, unfortunately, has been limited to wedding ceremonies only, 1 Corinthians 13:13 says, *"Now these three remain: faith, hope, and love. But the greatest of these is love."*

Many of our churches suffer from the same distraction as the Corinthians. Wanting to desperately know our "spiritual gift" from one of the lists in Paul's writings, we take surveys, inventories, and tests of all kind. Upon discovering what we might be gifted in, the temptation is to settle down into a ministry specific for it and rarely look up to see who God has put in our path that simply needs to be loved. Whether they know it or not, believers can become self-centered in simply trying to fulfill themselves by exercising their gift.

But love stands out. It is the driving force of not just our Christian ethic but of our whole life in Christ. Love is the environment in which God wishes to speak and act in our lives. Conducting our lives with the debt of love ensures us the right position to hear God's will.

Do you feel as if your supply of love is tapped out? Is there a demand for more but your tank is empty? *That* person in your life has used up all of your reserves—the person down the hallway at work, the neighbor down the block, or even your children at home. You know you ought to love them continually, but there doesn't seem to be any love left in your heart.

Now is the time for a change of definition for love. It is not a blend of our emotions, but the choice of who we owe. And we owe everyone love. It's a debt with no expiration date.

In Romans 13, after the charge to love, Paul begins to summarize the Law. But the Law appears too steep to ever be kept. Just keeping the Ten Commandments seems difficult. We normally avoid the "big" ones—murder, adultery, and stealing—but then we begin to struggle with the issues of lying and coveting what others have. When we consider all of the Law contained in the Old Testament, we are left with the feeling that no one could keep it.

Paul even quotes the very words of Jesus—*"You shall love your neighbor as yourself"* (Romans 13:9)—as a summation of the whole Law. Getting our neighbor's mail while she is on vacation is easy enough. Taking over food after a death in the family is not convenient, but we do it. Maybe even volunteering to babysit so a young couple can catch a break occasionally makes it into your calendar. But the idea that I would love the people next to my life as much as I value myself is a tough path to tread. We are surrounded by a lot of cranky and crazy people. But then again, when they look across the street at our house, they think the same thing.

To our advantage, we have the life of Christ poured out for our inability to fulfill the Law. The price required for us to escape judgment and enter intimacy with God is paid by the blood of Christ. If nothing else, our lives are to be a memorial honoring what Christ has done for us. His love poured out on our behalf gives life to our love for others. Jesus leaves no wiggle room when it comes to our lives of love: *"If you love Me, you will keep My commands"* (John 14:15). His commands in the Scriptures are pretty plain. It isn't hard to mine out the depths of His meaning. He says: *"If you keep My commands you will remain in My love, just as I have kept My Father's commands and remain in His love"* (John 15:10).

The closing chapters of the Gospel of John record the final moments of Jesus' life. He has gathered His closest followers in the Upper Room and has their enraptured attention. He speaks to them of the Comforter, fruit, and service. Yet the theme seems to be that of love. No doubt, Peter, Thomas, and the others had many questions about suffering and Christ's return. To them these would have been the more pressing issues. But Christ needs them to see that the motive of the heart is paramount in His work. His command is not in conquering the globe with an army or by forceful rhetoric. It is to change the world by love: searching, serving, dying love.

As we have the proper debt in focus, we can be on mission with Christ. But if the debt we carry is jealousy, then we don't desire what God has for us. When we carry the debt of a successful career, we have turned our lives away from the kingdom's agenda. If we choose an adrenaline rush as our debt, then we seek an artificial form of joy, rather than that of doing God's will. Today, choose to have the proper debt.

An eternal perspective: "The Day"

Besides this, knowing the time, it is already the hour for you to wake up from sleep, for now our salvation is nearer than when we first believed. The night is nearly over, and the daylight is near, so let us discard the deeds of darkness and put on the armor of light.

—ROMANS 13:11–12

The phrase "the daylight" used by Paul in this context has a specific usage. It refers to the time when Christ will appear again—the day of reckoning for humans and for history. Consummation of God's salvation will arrive at a specific time, literally on "the day." It should make us look ahead with a new and lengthened perspective of the future.

The eternal perspective we hold, however, can't be "pie in the sky." We need to see the days ahead and "the day" to come with an eye still on those around us. We shouldn't be so consumed with apocalyptic novels and endtime visions that we become useless to God in the here and now. Rather, with love being the fulfillment of the Law, we are to live with discernment regarding the end of days.

Ultimately, discernment about the present day always leads to an elongated perspective. We must understand our current times through the eyes of the kingdom. Random encounters are not random to God. Every phone call, conversation, and interaction has an eternal dimension.

When a first child is born into a young family, it changes your perspective on life. Certainly there are an overwhelming number of "right now" moments having to do with bottles, diapers, strollers, and sleepless nights. But caring for a child gives you a long-range perspective. She is small now, but not for long. Suddenly, the realization crashes into your life that you aren't raising a child; you're raising an adult. Your perspective changes.

Ultimately, discernment about the present day always leads to an elongated perspective. We should have that long-range perspective with how we live and move and breathe in the kingdom. We pour out love because it was lavished upon us by Christ. With love as the sole debt, our perspectives on people and days lengthen. Agitations are milder, and joys are stronger. Everyday occurrences are no longer pedestrian because there is more to them than the moment. Eternity hangs in the balance.

In athletics, coaches tweak daily drills in order to prepare the players for games that may not occur until the season's end. They want the team to be fully prepared. What I am learning right now may not be applicable for today, but God is refining my understanding in preparation for what is to come. His desire may be for the lesson I am learning now to be used in a week, a month, or a year.

That's why so many of the great saints of old kept copious notes in personal journals. You might be learning a lesson now that is intended for a mission much later. Philip remembers when the Lord used an older friend to alert him to 1 Samuel 2:35. It wasn't until two years later that he learned why: Some friends getting ready to go out on to the international missions field needed to hear about God's passion to have people faithful to His heart and mind. The eternal perspective causes us to ponder the lessons we are learning now so we are ready to hand them off to someone else when the time comes.

Jude 21 teaches us, *"Keep yourselves in the love of God, expecting the mercy of our Lord Jesus Christ for eternal life."* As we wait for the "period" to be put on the history books, wait in love. Experiencing God's presence through His expressions of love is an elemental factor of the believer's life which allows us to be fully prepared for what is yet to come.

Remember the book *Jim and Casper Go to Church* I referenced earlier? In this stinging account of the church today, Casper the atheist is puzzled by church greeters. It strikes him as odd that the entrances of churches are staffed by overly happy people lying in wait for visitors. He is convinced that no one—not even a Walmart greeter—is that happy to see a total stranger. To this one atheist, it seemed to be very contrived. Maybe, just maybe, he is right.

If you are a greeter at your church, please don't take offense at this. You recognize the need to be sincere in your Sunday morning ministry. But it is strange that at church, where love is the debt and eternity is the perspective, we feel it necessary to assign the "happy" people to the doors. If our churches were filled with people who adopted an eternal perspective of people, then whether it's Sunday or any other day, we would live differently. Everyone would greet with joy on Sundays. We would take more notice of the person who lived on the floor above us. Our eternal perspective—that God is bringing all things to an end, that the sheep will be separated from the goats, and that judgment will be final—should cause us to hold out love as the debt to everyone.

When Christ returns, it will be for a very different purpose than from His first appearance. Instead of slipping into humanity anonymously, He will arrive with great fanfare. His arrival at the Incarnation was as a quiet servant; at the Second Coming, it will be in unmistakable, undeniable victory. *"So also the Messiah, having been offered once to bear the sins of many, will appear a second time, not to bear sin, but to bring salvation to those who are waiting for Him"* (Hebrews 9:28).

When Christ comes again, it will not be to die but to bring consummation to our salvation. Our daily lives must be governed by the desire for God's glory to eternally be proclaimed. We can make that a reality as we prepare ourselves and others for "the day" that is sure to come. It will be the reality as we are pursued by God's love and as we pursue love toward others as the rule of God's agenda.

Transformed desires:
the life of Christ living in us

When you and I know God's agenda, we will be directed in such a way that our desires will be changed. The new birth changes our standing with God; His sanctifying work continuously transforms our aspirations. Conviction of sin brings painful indictment, and godliness brings soaring joy. The gospel metamorphosis should be ever taking hold of our desires.

*The night is nearly over, and the daylight is near, so let us discard
the deeds of darkness and put on the armor of light. Let us walk
with decency, as in the daylight: not in carousing and drunkenness;
not in sexual impurity and promiscuity; not in quarreling and*

jealousy. But put on the Lord Jesus Christ, and make
no plans to satisfy the fleshly desires.

—ROMANS 13:12–14

The battlefield imagery in this passage goes against the conventional wisdom regarding love. This Pauline passage of love is not about daisies and love letters. Instead it is a violent assault against evil. As we saw in the life of Christ earlier in chapter 3, we need to understand that love is not summed up in a romance novel or the latest romantic comedy movie. Love has emotions, but love is the battleground where God rescues the soul.

When we talk about love, it is not a weak emotional portent to submission of life. It is the strongest characteristic that can be in the human experience. Love speaks of the death to self. We speak of the strength of character as the compulsion for life as a missionary. Thus, we cast off the deeds of darkness and take upon ourselves the armor of light. Desires move from self-preservation to conformity of Jesus.

At the end of the movie version of J. R. R. Tolkien's "Lord of the Rings" Trilogy, we find Aragorn leading a small army at the end of *The Return of the King.* He is the rightful king and has come to assault the Black Gates of Mordor. Just the name of the evil city seems dark and ominous. These men have come to stand against what is dark, evil, and shallow of heart in Middle Earth. They have come to fight and, if necessary, to die for what is noble and good. Aragorn says to these men fitted for battle:

> "Hold your ground, hold your ground! Sons of Gondor, of Rohan, my brothers! I see in your eyes the same fear that would take the heart of me. A day may come when the courage of men fails, when we forsake our friends and break all bonds of fellowship, but it is not this day. An hour of woes and shattered shields, when the age of men comes crashing down! But it is not this day! This day we fight! By all that you hold dear on this good Earth, I bid you stand, Men of the West!"

In this moment, the men following Aragorn decide to love the cause that is greater than themselves. By doing so, they are transformed into heroes.

Battlefield language is appropriate when it comes to transforming our desires. It is not easy to change what we love. It is time, though, to stand our ground. Bitterness, anger, and foul language are much easier when we are stuck in a traffic jam and some jerk is trying to change three lanes at once. Giving oneself over to what is pleasurable for the moment is more along the liking of our flesh than to submit to the life of Christ that is growing within. Too often we are like the pig at the trough whose singular thought is to gorge itself. We find ourselves fat, but still hungry. Thus, the war must be waged to convert our desires. Our desires are no small pets to tame; rather, they are beasts to slay.

When we are properly suited, the armor of light is a protective covering that allows us to see and act according to the character of Christ. His eternal perspective of those around us becomes our own vision. Protecting His reputation and lifting up His glory becomes the weightiest duty of our day— and the most joyous.

If we are to *"put on the Lord Jesus Christ"* (Romans 13:14), then we need an image. One such image is the beautiful portrait in Philippians 2:5–11 of Christ's humility unto death for our sake.

Too often, the lesson ends there. Christ is beautiful in His humble death. A lesson about Christ is taught here that gives us a greater appreciation of our Lord's servant nature. God had more in mind for the Philippians and us. The following verses speak of its application to us.

"So then, my dear friends, just as you have always obeyed, not only in my presence, but now even more in my absence, work out your own salvation with fear and trembling. For it is God who is working in you, enabling you both to desire and to work out His good purpose."

—Philippians 2:12–13

We are commanded to *"work out"* our salvation to look more and more like the Suffering Servant. This takes a candid recognition that God is accomplishing this work. It also requires a steadfast heart ready for change. Therefore we must humble ourselves as Christ did. His mission was to bow even to death.

There is a dangerous prayer you should consider carefully before praying: "Lord, break me." These three words are not to be uttered glibly or without thought about what might follow.

Psalm 51 is a great place to begin if we find ourselves needing to be conformed to God's heart. This is reportedly the response of King David when he was confronted about his adultery with Bathsheba. Verses 7–8 give us insight into the process God may take with us: *"Purify me with hyssop, and I will be clean; wash me, and I will be whiter than snow. Let me hear joy and gladness; let the bones You have crushed rejoice."*

Obviously, we welcome the tenderness of being cleansed with the fragrant hyssop, but we aren't so sure about having our bones crushed by God! Even so, we should welcome the good work of God to conform us to the image of Christ by exorcising all sin from us. Let there be no mistaking in what is taught: to live out the mission of God is to take upon the desire of Christ that He was willing to exhaust His life upon. The selfish deeds of darkness consume energy for self. Operating missionally translates into a new character released from the burdens of self-gratification or fulfilling the Law. It is freed to live for the fame of Christ among the nations.

Moving from destination to destiny

The question, *What is God's will for my life?*, holds more promise than fear. With a better understanding of God's mission, it has become a welcome friend in my life, because I realize the opportunity God presents in it to discover the character of Christ being formed in me. By seeking an answer to it, I can find my place in His mission.

Though heaven is included, salvation is not about a destination. It is the call to intimacy with the One Who is God. He has chosen us as His friends (John 15:14). As we seek to do the will of God according to a missionary calling in this world, we begin at the beginning—the incredible entryway made for us into the holy of holies. Where fear reigned due to the justice of God, now loving assurance abounds because of His welcoming bidding for us to come and dine at the King's table. Knowing the will of God must always begin with knowing the God who wills.

Here are the lyrics to Keith Green's "I Want to Be More Like Jesus":

> As each day passes by, I feel my love run dry
> I get so weary, worn and tossed 'round in
>   the storm
> Well I'm blind to all His needs and I'm tired
>   of planting seeds
> I seem to have a wealth of so many thoughts
>   about myself
>
> I want to, I need to, be more like Jesus
> I want to, I need to, be more like Him
>
> Our Father's will was done by giving us His Son
> Who paid the highest cost, to point us
>   to the cross.
> And when I think of Him taking on the whole
>   world's sin
> I take one look at me compared to what I'm
>   called to be
>
> I want to, I need to, be more like Jesus.
> I want to, I need to, be more like Him.
> Remember, there's no greater love
> Than to lay down your life for a friend
>
> The end of all my prayers is to care like
>   my Lord cares

My one and only goal, His image in my soul
Yes, my weakness is revealed when by His stripes
    I'm healed
He's faithful and He's true to complete the work
    He begins in you

Points for Personal Reflection and Group Discussion

1. Reflecting on the last few months of your life, what have been some of the more obvious directions that God has given to you?

2. What areas of God's revealed will (the Scriptures) are the easiest for you to follow right now? What are the more difficult?

3. List all of the debts you have in your checkbook. Which seems more pressing: financial debts or the spiritual debt of love? Why?

4. What do you think of when considering the end of the world? Do you look at it with fear or anticipation?

5. What elements are necessary to change your perspective of people from temporary to eternal?

6. Read Ephesians 6:10–18. In the battle with our flesh, what parts of the "armor of God" should you be more diligent in putting on?

7. Discuss how operating missionally will enable you to live more like Jesus according to Philippians 2:5–13.

8. What needs do you seem to notice over and over again? Take time to consider and discuss if God is calling you into a mission activity to touch a certain need, people group, or part of the world.

Chapter 12

CALLED TO LOVE

LIVING A MISSIONARY PASSION
FOR THE LOST

During one of my church plants, I hauled the needed equipment for services to the high school cafeteria in my Ford Explorer Sport Trac, or as my friends call it, my *girlie* truck. For some reason, when my daughter Kristen was eight years old, she thought she was needed at the 7:00 a.m. setup. One morning, after setting up chairs for a while, she suddenly stopped. She walked over to me, put her hands on her hips, and asked, "Do you know why we set up the chairs?"

I thought it was obvious; we were setting up for church . . . but I smelled a trap. So I simply said, "For church?" She said, "Nope, so people can come and hear about Jesus." And she was right.

Even during the elementary school ages, her love for people showed through her desire to share her faith—which she did one day with our Jewish neighbors. Kristen invited Allison (not her real name) to church, which her parents didn't appreciate. Our family reads Scripture and prays before dinner every night and it's no different when we have neighborhood kids over . . . so Kristen knows talking about your faith with those who don't know Christ is just normal.

One day while Kristen was with Allison, she shared with her about Jesus. Her parents weren't interested or appreciative. At some point in their talking, Kristen must have mentioned "the lake of fire." Those exact words aren't usual in our home, so I am not sure if it's an accurate rendition—but I sure did hear about it from Allison's parents.

That conversation led to one of the oddest father-daughter talks of my life. I had to tell my daughter to be careful in how she shared her faith. Allison's parents wanted Kristen to stop talking about Jesus and stop sharing her faith. I couldn't go that far, but I encouraged her to show her faith rather than just tell it. But, her question was pretty clear, "Why would I not want to tell her?"

Funny, that seems quite the opposite of what I often hear from many church people. Their love for Christ often doesn't lead to a love for their lost neighbors—or at least not enough to tell them the important truth. To quote Kristen, "Why would I not want to tell?"

GOD'S MISSIONAL PASSION

Jonah—reluctant missionary

The story of Jonah is one that little church kids learn early on. It is like a Disney story in the Bible. Jonah begins innocently enough—as far as prophets' lives go. God tells him to go and warn the people of the coming judgment, but God didn't send Jonah to his chosen people. Rather, he is to warn Israel's mortal enemies, the Assyrians, of God's impending judgment on them.

So, instead of heading due east to Nineveh, Jonah boards a ship and heads due west. His intention is to sail to Tarshish, as far away from Nineveh as he can get. This is where it gets wild. God sends a violent storm to disrupt his escape plan. The pagan sailors discover Jonah is the cause of the calamity, and the ship is about to sink. Jonah suggests they toss him overboard so only he will perish at sea.

But God has a strange redemption plan in mind for Jonah—three days in the stomach of a giant fish. In fact, the movie *Pinocchio* puts on film what we imagine must have been the case for Jonah (Jonah 2). But here, instead of Gepetto searching for his boy, we have the prophet running from God. We are given a glimpse of Jonah's prayer life, which seems to be increasing rapidly. The prayer ends with Jonah's declaration, *"But as for me, I will sacrifice to You with a voice of thanksgiving. I will fulfill what I have vowed. Salvation is from the Lord!"* (Jonah 2:9)

At this point, Jonah is burped up onto dry ground and God again commands him to go and speak His message to the Ninevites (Jonah 3:2). This time, Jonah goes.

The third chapter of Jonah focuses on the Ninevites' response to the warning that God is going to show up. They receive the short message: *"In 40 days Nineveh will be demolished"* (Jonah 3:4). This message predicted the loss of what is most precious to their capital city—self-rule.

Yet, the king, his court, and all of the people respond appropriately—they repent. There is mourning over sin, fasting in prayer, and a lot of calling on God in the streets of Nineveh. The beauty of God's love is shown again as the chapter concludes in 3:10: *"Then God saw their actions—that they had turned from their evil ways—so God relented from the disaster He had threatened to do to them. And He did not do it."*

They repented and God relented.

Now, the fourth chapter brings us back to our old friend Jonah. One would think he would be leading a worship service for the Ninevites to celebrate God's mercy and proclaim His salvation. But he is not. He left the city in a huff. Jonah was angry because God did not destroy the enemies of his people.

Mark Driscoll observed, Jonah's response "brings us all under the conviction that we love the things God has given us (homes, cars, hobbies, health, friends, etc.) more than the great city and it's spiritually blind people who we pass every day and ignore because our minds are consumed with trivia and angrily pondering about how unfair God is."[1]

We are Jonah

If Jonah's heart disturbs us, then perhaps we should allow this story to serve as a place for accountability regarding our own view of the lost. The Book of Jonah is not about the geopolitics of the ancient world, but reveals God's agenda for a great and influential city. His agenda reveals the depth of His grace.

Honestly, I sometimes struggle with being in vocational ministry. It's not that I don't love God or that I want to be disobedient. I struggle because dealing with people on a spiritual level is messy. Sometimes people are mean, cynical, and stubborn about their religious opinions. I love the ministry, but it is all the people who mess it up!

Jonah probably loves the fact that God loves Jonah's people. He knows the story of God's deliverance during the Exodus and His power at the walls of Jericho. Jonah is aware of God's power to provide a glorious future, but he only wants it for the right people. Jonah loves God's love—as long as it is applied in a manner acceptable to him.

Overcoming Obstacles

Being indwelt by God's Spirit should inspire a passion for the lost. He is a guard against any cynicism toward the people in our culture. Most people today are quite open to spiritual things, but they are cynical about the church. We are seen as rigid and judgmental, self-absorbed, and apathetic to real social needs, caring only about our own. While many unbelievers mobilize to meet the needs of those who lack clean drinking water, need help after tsunamis, or need to be rescued from modern slavery, they perceive that the church has rested on its laurels of ages past.

It is possible that we've failed to see people through God's eyes. We are not passionate toward the lost; we lack love and compassion. We turn away from noticing real needs of even our closest neighbors.

We need to consider whether we, like Jonah, are reluctant to share God's message of repentance out of our fear, anger at those outside our faith, or for other reasons. Do we care about the lost? Are we willing to let God demonstrate His love through us? With love as a compelling force for our mission, let's look at the end of Jonah's story.

Jonah's heart—4:1

All children are capable of pitching a fit. Some are just better at it than others. It is an innate reaction to not getting one's way. Jonah successfully pulls off pitching a fit right in the face of God.

As he storms out of Nineveh to the east side of the city, he is furious with God and levels his complaint against Him. He stamps his feet in the presence of deity. He is pouting at the One whose words are life. Scowling at Yahweh just does not seem like a good idea to me, but his heart is filled with two emotions. *"But Jonah was greatly displeased and became furious"* (Jonah 4:1).

Anger

The anger he developed was not a mild frustration. This was a burning, white-hot emotion in his soul. Most of us, at some point or another, have been so angry we could "spit nails." Jonah was there.

Jonah was angry because he desired religious validation for his people alone. He knew what would happen if he went to Nineveh. He knew God would forgive those who repented. Well aware of God's history of redemption with Israel, he knew God is One who withholds judgment when people repent and submit to Him. Jonah fled from his Nineveh assignment not because he feared the people but in knowing God might save them.

In his childish tantrum, Jonah wanted Israel to be the only ones validated as God's people. The Assyrians had risen up against Israel many times in battle. They had called on their pagan deities to help them slaughter his countrymen. The prophet Nahum describes Nineveh as a *"city of blood, totally deceitful, full of plunder, never without prey"* in Nahum 3:1.

They had killed so many that the dead piled up and people stumbled over them (Nahum 3:3). The Assyrians were a wicked people who were unworthy of redemption. In the eyes of someone like Jonah, these people were beyond the reach of grace. But then again, aren't we all? Even Jonah.

Jonah took an absurd position against God. He was ticked off that the king of the Ninevites has led his people to repent. So, he pitched his fit and sulked a while.

Selfish

But Jonah's heart was not just angry; it was also selfish. Beyond religious validation solely for his people, Jonah wanted personal vindication. The role of the prophet in the Old Testament is simple—deliver God's message and be right. And Jonah thinks he's been played for a fool.

The simple message God gives Jonah to deliver is recorded in Jonah 3:4, *"In 40 days Nineveh will be demolished!"* It was the worst possible scenario for the Ninevites. They would lose power over the capital city of the empire—the best of all possibilities in the mind of Jonah. He was looking for the "lightning-bolt-from-heaven" moment, hoping for the same fire and brimstone that rained down upon Sodom and Gomorrah. Like their marauding army had done to others, Jonah was hoping for God to wipe them off the face of the earth.

What Jonah missed was that Nineveh *had been* overturned. He wanted to be vindicated by boldly proclaiming God's message and witnessing a violent execution of judgment. A city overthrown in terms prescribed by a prophet of doom was his hope. Instead, God's arrival and Nineveh's overthrow is accomplished with a surrendering king and a mourning people. Rather than destruction, there is redemption. And Jonah does not like it.

Eugene Peterson used Jonah as a template for a book regarding pastoral ministry. Regarding Jonah's fourth chapter, he describes the contrast between Jonah and God. He says, "Jonah had a child-sized plan that did not pan out; whereas God had a hugely dimensioned destiny that surprised everyone when it was enacted."[2] Jonah was like a child misunderstanding the greater plan of God.

The followers of Christ were much the same. When Christ faced opposition from the Samaritans, James and John wanted to step up to the plate and take care of these rabble-rousers for Jesus. They asked Jesus in Luke 9:54, *"Lord, do You want us to call down fire from heaven to consume them?"* It doesn't take a scholar to guess the Lord's reaction—stern rebuke. They have no idea what they are asking. Their religious zeal and selfish need for vindication has overshadowed God's desire for mercy.

A quick look at the eighth chapter of Acts reveals what is to come for the Samaritans—a citywide revival led by Philip, a sorcerer saved and so much spiritual fruit that Peter and John are sent from Jerusalem to help out. The religious duty John desired, out of bravado, would have decimated the work that was to come later.

Peterson says Jonah "thought he had come to Nineveh to do a religious job, to administer a religious program. God had brought Jonah to Nineveh to give him an experience of amazing grace."[3] We need to drop our egotistical needs when God is trying to engage us in His redemptive work of saving the people in our city.

God's heart

Jonah's heart is difficult for us to handle. It seems too much of a mirror to our own soul on the days we deal with the difficult and the unlovable. Yet, from the mouth and in the prayer of this childish prophet, there comes one of the great theological declarations in all of the Old Testament. Unfortunately he seems unable to make a personal application of the truth.

*He prayed to the Lord: "Please, Lord, isn't this what I said while I
was still in my own country? That's why I fled toward Tarshish in
the first place. I knew that You are a merciful and compassionate
God, slow to become angry, rich in faithful love,
and One who relents from sending disaster."*

—JONAH 4:2

God chose to reach the Ninevites despite their sinfulness and Jonah's reluctance. But even though Jonah admits his wrongdoing in running from God's work, he is stalwart in his rebellion. Yet, as God reached out to Nineveh, we see the heart that should be ours.

Caring

The first phrase regarding God's heart is *"merciful and compassionate."* God's love stands directly opposite to Jonah's hatred. Jonah wants an Old Testament smiting to occur. But God shows benevolence to the undeserving sinners in Nineveh. You and I know the feeling. Jonah had grown callous to it.

God's grace has a certain depth to it we often miss. On the surface, we see an offering of goodwill or reconciliation; but behind it, there lies a favorable disposition by the offended party toward the offenders. The only motivation for such an attitude is that of love freely given with no hope of repayment.

The Hebrew word for compassion is as the care a mother shows to her child. A mom's ability to get to her child at the moment of need is astonishing. Moms have an amazing facility for deciphering a confusion of sounds and discerning the cries of their little ones over all the others. Moms can gather up a wounded child to tend to his or her needs unlike any other. And the child will often tell you that they want their mommy instead of anyone else. A mother's heart is often one of undying compassion.

When God speaks to Jonah at the end of the book, He asks Jonah about the 120,000 Ninevites who do not know their right hand from their left. Would Jonah have God leave them to their own devices to find redemption? God's heart is far too great for such a callous action. He intervenes by overthrowing their self-governing power so that He might benevolently heal their sin-scarred lives.

Sadly, the Book of Jonah ends with Jonah still pouting. It isn't recorded that God used him again. It is a dangerous thing to be disqualified for ministry because of anger, bitterness, or unwillingness to submit to God's will. When we pout, we are only usable as an example of how not to engage God's mission.

Forgiving

Jonah points out that God is *"slow to become angry, rich in faithful love"* (Jonah 4:2). Do you hesitate in anger or do you have a quick fuse? Fortunately for us, Jesus was willing to put up with our shortcomings for what seems to be an excruciating amount of time. As it is expressed in old language, our Lord is "long-suffering."

A lesson in Hebrew is necessary here. You realize by now that the English word *love* does not often do justice to the concept because we apply it so widely and indiscriminately. In this verse, a specific Hebrew word is used for love: *hesed*. It's not the love between friends nor is it the love of two spouses. Rather, this is the covenant love God has shown to Israel. *Hesed* is the love expressed to Abraham, the father of Jonah's people. In covenantal love, a deal is struck and nothing can prevent God from fulfilling His word. When Jonah moves from the word of compassion to this term of contractual love, he is expressing the trustworthy nature of God's love.

God is prepared to show the same type of love to the Ninevites that He has shown to the Israelites. In Jonah's mind, this scandalous idea offers hope for the Assyrian Empire. God will be their God, and they will be His people. Jonah must have taken personal offense to that scenario. For the enemies of God to be treated with as much mercy as the Israelites implies both need the same divine assistance.

God offer of forgiveness to the degenerates of this city puts our own lives in perspective. Like Jonah, we enjoy being the apple of God's eye. But like the older brother in the parable of the prodigal son, an ego problem is at work.

I have often wondered about "foxhole" conversions. Whether they're actually on the battlefield or lying on one's death bed, the last-minute conversion seems a bit unfair to the rest of us.

For example, Philip became a Christian at the age of seven. He still has his childhood Bible where his father wrote down the phrase "Philip W. Nation II became a Christian on July 31, 1977." He has been working out his salvation for over 30 years. Is it fair that someone who is saved at the very end of an old life, even a sin-filled life, would receive the same covenant of grace Philip has enjoyed?

From a human perspective, the answer is no. But God is not bound to our way of thinking. From the divine perspective of whether a foxhole decision is fair, the answer is yes. Why? Because we are all lawbreakers.

Some find fault in God's plan to redeem people at various stages of life and out of what we view as significantly vile lives. Jonah certainly finds disparity in God's plan, but God's love for the remorseful Ninevites far outweighs Jonah's misshapen sense of justice.

Redeeming

The Ninevites repented, and God withheld the judgment they rightly deserved. Our Lord is *"One who relents from sending disaster"* (Jonah 4:2). But this is the view we all wish to have if we dare to turn our gaze toward heaven.

The gavel has dropped. A harsh sentence is about to finalized. Yet the hand of the judge is stayed. A life is spared. Only through the intervention of someone with greater authority can this be the case. In the spiritual realm, only God can make such an intervention.

The question that Jonah leaves us to ponder is who would we be if God simply left us to ourselves and stopped pursuing us? The answer is not pleasant. For those in the faith, we would resemble the stereotype of the church prevalent in today's culture. We would in fact become selfish, inwardly focused, judgmental religious hacks. The destiny for those outside the faith is even worse. They would be left without hope to eternally perish in their sin.

So what can be done to stem the tide of selfish behavior? We must take upon ourselves the heart of God for the people around us. We certainly do not want the hard-line position taken by Jonah that God is a God of wrath for all those dissimilar to himself.

We need the heart of God in order to live out the mission of God. Conversely, we need to be on the mission of God in order to understand His heart. Both are necessary. But beware of the religious activity that keeps you so busy that you never encounter God's heart for those who are far from Him.

Paul's heart—missionary extraordinaire

Perhaps one of the best examples we can see is that of the Apostle Paul. In his life, we see a mortal man assume upon himself the position that the only thing that really matters is the gospel. Paul's life challenges us to take a heart inventory as to our passion for the "Ninevites" around us. Do we desire God's agenda of loving redemption on their behalf?

Ambition

US President Theodore Roosevelt once said:

"Far better it is to dare mighty things, to win glorious triumphs, even though checkered by failure, than to rank with those poor spirits who neither enjoy much nor suffer much, because they live in that gray twilight that knows neither victory nor defeat." In this light, I want you to think of ambition as a virtue. It is a driving force pressing us toward a higher goal.

Our culture's heroes display an ambition for personal greatness. The Scriptures' heroes, however, burn with ambition for another's glory. The Apostle Paul wrote, *"My aim is to evangelize where Christ has not been named, so that I will not build on someone else's foundation"* (Romans 15:20). This verse stands as the slogan for many missionaries and church planters. Our desire is take the gospel where it is unknown to the masses. The impact of the verse rightly draws us to plow up the soil of human hearts so that the first seed of the gospel may be deposited.

A few years ago, Philip traveled into the Middle East with some friends. While there, he visited with the faculty and students of an Arab seminary in

Beirut, Lebanon. Yes—you read that right. There is a Christian seminary in the middle of Beirut! The students at the seminary come from numerous countries where Islam is the majority religion and most of them have faced severe persecution. However, what Philip found most humbling was that they were all planning on returning home upon graduation. Knowing they would face harassment, arrests, and possibly worse, they still had the ambition to plant the gospel in places where it was not known.

Paul has this same thought. But the impact of "ambition" takes it to a whole other level. If we sat down with a child and asked about his or her ambitions, it would remind us of our own childhood. We might hear dreams of being a fighter pilot or an actress. Children tell us they want to be rich, loved, famous, and powerful. Our ambitions may include being well received by others, respected, or even feared. Maybe there's a novel you always wanted to write or produce an invention that everyone in the world needs. Maybe you plan to visit the Great Wall of China or scuba dive at the Great Barrier Reef. Ambitions are very much like compulsions—they determine our behavior.

Paul is captured by a new ambition. His life is now deeply rooted in the gospel. His ambition is to make Christ famous among the nations and see transformation in the lives of believers. In Paul we see the heart of God working itself out in the life of a man.

Passion

Paul has a goal for the gospel to be made known in every corner of the world. His goal will be driven by his passion for others. Note the extreme nature of his impassioned plea for others to be saved: "*For I could almost wish to be cursed and cut off from the Messiah for the benefit of my brothers, my own flesh and blood*" (Romans 9:3).

Our high school English teachers taught us about hyperbole—making an exaggerated statement in order to evoke strong emotions. Theologically, Paul knows he cannot be "cut off from the Messiah." His epistles hold some of the strongest revelations from God regarding the security of our salvation.

Nevertheless, his passion is so great for his unsaved countrymen that he says he would surrender his own salvation if they could be saved.

This is the true heart of our Savior upon the Cross. Hanging there in a spiritual agony far outweighing any physical torture, He cries out in Mark 15:34, *"My God, my God, why have You forsaken Me?"* In this moment, as He becomes the sin offering for humanity, Christ is cut off from His relationship to the Father.

We can't presume to understand this moment in the act of redemption—relationship interrupted over the passion for humanity's salvation—but Paul seeks to reflect this passion. In this man beats an intensity of heart that would do anything, go anywhere, and suffer any consequence for the sake of the gospel.

The passion of Jonah is about personal validation and religious positioning. Paul's passion is surrendering a life of political power so that he might gain his soul. We face two paths and must choose the one in which our whole being is given over for the gospel's effect on the great city God has placed us in.

What now?

It would be easy to end this chapter with a nice rah-rah cheer, wave our pom-poms, and get excited about Jesus. That's not enough. We need to apply this message to our hearts. What could we actually do to have this type of heart? Don't be fooled. It is not mission until it moves from our heart to our hands.

Here are a few suggestions for making this happen in our churches.

First, we can pray to see people as God sees them. We have a tendency merely to walk by the harvest field. We must begin to see the people around us in terms of whether they have a relationship with God. We must see those without this relationship, as God sees them—harassed and helpless, like sheep without a shepherd (Matthew 9:36). We should rightly see that Jesus did not evade the world but invaded it and consequently places us "out here" as an outpost for His kingdom.

Second, we can pray for those in our churches, starting with our Bible study group, whether it is a Sunday School class, missions group, women's group, or men's fellowship. But we can go beyond keeping a private prayer journal. We want to actually tell our friends we are praying for them.

Next, we can go out and discover a real need in someone else's life. Once we know what it is, we can do everything in our power to meet that need. We should not do it because of a guilty conscience for past apathy. Rather, we should allow the Spirit of God to kindle our passion for that person's condition before God. Then, as we find ourselves driven to love the lost, meeting their needs as a bridge for the gospel will become natural and enjoyable.

Finally, and decidedly important, tell someone. Prayer and service are ways that we pave a clear path for the gospel to be told, discussed, or even debated. The mission for which we are so compelled to participate in is to make disciples. To do so, people who are far from understanding the gospel need to hear a true representation of it. We must find our way toward emulating the heart and life of Paul who was willing to give all so people loved could know the truth of Christ. So pray and serve, but be sure to go and tell.

Points for Personal Reflection and Group Discussion

1. Discuss some prevailing ambitions evident in today's culture.

2. What are some of the ambitions that have driven you in the past, both the positive and negative?

3. Have you ever become angry with God because He did not answer a prayer as you had hoped He would? What did you learn about His plans after you settled down?

4. Discuss the three descriptors of God's heart for the Ninevites: caring, forgiving, and redemptive. How can we offer these to those for whom God cares?

5. We have all failed at times. Do you remember a time when someone refused to give up on you?

6. Do you feel as if you are serving in the city of Nineveh? What can you do to make a difference?

7. How can you change the mentality of your church to move away from the heart of Jonah and pursue the heart of God, as illustrated in the Apostle Paul's life?

8. Who is in your life right now that needs to hear a verbal witness about how your life has been changed by the gospel?

CONCLUSION

Love hurts, love scars,

Love wounds, and marks,

Any heart, not tough,

Or strong, enough

To take a lot of pain,

Take a lot of pain

Love is like a cloud

Holds a lot of rain

Love hurts, ooh ooh love hurts

. . .

Ooh ooh love hurts

"Love Hurts"
written by Boudleaux Bryant
© 1960 by House of Bryant Publications
USED BY PERMISSION
ALL RIGHTS RESERVED

So begins one of those songs that stick with you for life—and this one has been significant to me since the mid-70s.1 I lived in Levittown, just outside New York City, and like everyone else my age, we just understood there were certain ballads that *needed* to be sung—*loudly*. And, "Ooh ooh love hurts" was one of those.

In Levittown, 1975 was a tough year. The place had seen better days, and I remember collecting hypodermic needles left on the sidewalk (much to the horror of my parents). A huge fire broke out at the World Trade Center, confirming my grandfather's decree that my mother should never work there.

In New York City, what many called the "liberal experiment" of American neosocialism was coming to an end—rapidly. The social spending had simply become too much. NYC was headed toward bankruptcy. President Ford didn't want to help, leading to one of the most famous headlines of all time: "Ford to City: Drop Dead."

Public services fell apart, so my grandfather figured it was time to get out and moved to Florida. He wasn't alone; a million people moved out of NYC that year. My family followed my grandfather two years later in hope of finding work and a better life. My father couldn't find work in New York; there wasn't much use for union Ironworker's Local # 46 NYC when no one was building. He'd sobered up in 1971, turned his life around, but still couldn't find work. Yes, 1975 was a tough year. It was the year I stopped signing cards, "Love, Ed."

Love does hurt, but a life without it hurts even worse. When we live a life without love, and claim to be a Christian, it's bad for us and it's bad for the cause of Christ.

My prayer is that the portrait of love presented in this book will encourage you to live a life compelled by the love of Christ. As you access additional study material in *The Mission of God* Study Bible from pastors, church planters, vocational missionaries, and other church leaders, I hope that you will both learn and live out this love by Christ. Our lives are not to be the same once we begin to mine the depths of Christ's love. Ours is to be a life formed from God's missional heart. It's a life filled with the activity of God's missional body—the church. And it's a life that transforms you into a missionary for God.

But I've deliberately not given you a definition of love. Why? Because love is impossible to fully define. Though I'd like to offer a pithy, insightful definition for love, it would simply be foolish. Love is part of God's character. It's also a human emotion. Love is mystical but also practical. Love is a choice and oftentimes a compulsion. Love's true nature is beyond my comprehension.

But my prayer is that you will come to a deeper understanding of God and His great love. I've learned to pray this for my wife, children, family, and friends. Now it is my prayer for you. As you've taken the journey to discover something about the why of missional ministry, I hope that in the process you've discovered the very heart of the kingdom of God that seeks to extend the glory of God to all creation. And love is one of God's greatest means for such a beautiful task.

In Ephesians 3:14–21, the Apostle Paul tells a young church that he has prayed for them. Even better, he tells them what he prayed on their behalf:

For this reason I kneel before the Father from whom every family in heaven and on earth is named. I pray that He may grant you, according to the riches of His glory, to be strengthened with power in the inner man through His Spirit, and that the Messiah may dwell in your hearts through faith. I pray that you, being rooted and firmly established in love, may be able to comprehend with all the saints what is the length and width, height and depth of God's love, and to know the Messiah's love that surpasses knowledge, so you may be filled with all the fullness of God. Now to Him who is able to do above and beyond all that we ask or think according to the power that works in us—to Him be glory in the church and in Christ Jesus to all generations, forever and ever. Amen.

Love plays a major role in Paul's intercession for that church. I want to encourage you to adopt this prayer for your life or, if you are a church leader, for your entire church this year. It will help you to focus on being pursued by and pursuing the love of God.

A theological prayer

Paul invokes ideas of Father, Son, and Spirit in the opening words. We are created by the Father, empowered by the Spirit, and have Christ's presence as a resident within us. Paul asked the Lord to strengthen the new believers by the power of the Spirit living in them. All this is to lovingly draw us into His work and agenda. As we abide in Christ's loving presence, He will certainly use the fruit of new converts and renewed character only His redemption can offer.

An idealistic prayer

Paul could have ended his prayer in the middle of verse 17, and it still would have been an impressive prayer. But he goes on to pray for the presence of God to affect lives in an intensely personal manner—that love would be known.

Rather than describing love again here, he simply says it is boundless. In 1 Corinthians 13, Paul took a practical look at love. There he gave insight to the patient, humble, protective love we should give and desire to receive. He even made the bold statements that "love never fails" (v. 8 NIV) and it reigns supreme over faith and hope (v. 13).

For the Ephesians, there is a different approach. It is the same I would leave with you. After having described, parsed, and illustrated love in the Godhead, the church, and your life, we should all wonder where the boundary of love is. But love's boundaries are like the horizons—always out of reach.

Love is to be our establishment and foundation; but from that concrete foundation, love's effect transcends our ability to appreciate. Though we *love* love, we too often desire to have command of it. People tend to domesticate everything—including love.

So Paul prays that believers might receive the power *"to comprehend with all the saints what is the length and width, height and depth of God's love"* (Ephesians 3:18). The love of God is beyond our insights to comprehend, and its boundaries are beyond our ability to see. But the prayer asks for the Ephesians to understand the expansive nature of God's love. It's a seemingly impossible request. And without the presence of God's Spirit and the indwelling love of Christ, we would be like children playing with the space shuttle at NASA. Yet we know his prayer comes from a heart filled with faith in the God who can accomplish all things.

Paul's prayer is that our minds would begin to conceive the inconceivable. He wants us to know what is unknowable. Love—which dwells in the infinite spiritual realm—is to be known by finite creation. Perhaps we have thought that the greatest act of God's love is that He would teach us what love is. But it isn't. The greatest act of God's love is that He would teach us *who He is.*

Love, so powerful in our lives and so expansive in its scope, is created by the Lord so we can know the fullness of His character. We should desire to *"be filled with all the fullness of God"* (v. 19). We do not come to idealize love. Rather, Jesus uses love to idealize His presence within us.

We don't reach the limit of love; we only reach the limit of our ability to hold it. Our fullness is not nearly all the love there is; it's just all we can hold.

An expectant prayer

I have always been interested in how people end their prayers. Some conclude like landing a plane on a long runway—easy and smooth. Other endings are more like landing on an aircraft carrier—a sudden jolt. Paul concluded his prayer for the Ephesians with a hope for the miraculous.

When God's love takes hold of a person, the extraordinary occurs. It's not due to the one to whom love has been revealed. The Revealer is the one who is able to unfold the infinite possibilities when love interrupts our reality. Paul prayed, *"Now to Him who is able to do above and beyond all that we ask or think according to the power that works in us—to Him be glory in the church and in Christ Jesus to all generations, forever and ever. Amen"* (Ephesians 3:20–21).

Let me just admit, I love that benediction. I am enraptured by it because it so succinctly states my own hope. I earnestly desire for the colossal power of God to be at work in my narrow existence.

Every day, we face minor and major skirmishes. Our battles are waged in homes and across kitchen tables, in cubicles and across conference room tables. It often seems as if we live in a narrow slice of life, making it difficult to see beyond the end of the day and our lists of things to do. Yet we want to see the power of God at work, and we want to join Him in a mission that will take us beyond human imagination.

My hope is that this book already has your imagination churning. Hopefully, you're learning about answers to your problems, questions, and even skepticism.

But here's the great news—the good news: God will move us further into the work of His mission than we could possibly dream! It is His intention that we not just hear about what He is doing but be a participant in the work of redemption and restoration in our world.

Paul prays for believers to be strengthened so we will have the power to understand God's love. He asks for the unimaginable power of God to be active in our lives. And his final request is that the glory of God would be realized beyond description. Paul's expectant prayer was not just for cool God stuff to happen that fixes our problems. Too much is at stake. True desire finds its fulfillment when the glory of God prevails over the earth and throughout every generation.

And that is my prayer for you. Let love find its place in the expansion of God's glory and reign over the entire earth and all its peoples.

APPENDIX

APPENDIX—THE PATH TO SALVATION

As you have read this book, perhaps you have come to the conclusion that you have not yet given Christ first place in your life. Please carefully study the following and it will guide you to understand and received God's salvation offered to you in love.

Salvation—identify with Christ

"Now I make known to you, brethren, the gospel which I preached to you, which also you received, in which also you stand, by which also you are saved, if you hold fast the word which I preached to you, unless you believed in vain. For I delivered to you as of first importance what I also received, that Christ died for our sins according to the Scriptures, and that He was buried, and that He was raised on the third day according to the Scriptures." 1 Corinthians 15:1–4 (NASB)

You Must Start with a Right Understanding

Of God and Creation

- "In the beginning God created the heavens and the earth" (Genesis 1:1).
- "So God created man in his own image, in the image of God he created him; male and female he created them" (Genesis 1:27 NIV).
- "You are worthy, our Lord and God, to receive glory and honor and power, for you created all things, and by your will they were created and have their being" (Revelation 4:11 NIV).
- "They are my people—I created each of them to bring honor to me" (Isaiah 43:7 CEV).

Of the Fall

- "Therefore, just as sin entered the world through one man, and death through sin, and in this way death came to all men, because all sinned." (Romans 5:12 NIV)
- For as in Adam all die, so in Christ all will be made alive" (1 Corinthians 15:22 NIV).

Of Jesus as Creator and Redeemer

- "Worthy is the Lamb, who was slain, to receive power and wealth and wisdom and strength and honor and glory and praise! Then I heard every creature in heaven and on earth and under the earth and on the sea, and all that is in them, singing: "To him who sits on the throne and to the Lamb be praise and honor and glory and power, for ever and ever!'" (Revelation 5:12–13 NIV).

Of Jesus and His Death

- "For God so loved the world that he gave his one and only Son, that whoever believes in him shall not perish but have eternal life" (John 3:16 NIV).

- "He was delivered over to death for our sins and was raised to life for our justification" (Romans 4:25 NIV).

- "But God demonstrates his own love for us in this: While we were still sinners, Christ died for us" (Romans 5:8 NIV).

Of Self

- "There is no one righteous, not even one; there is no one who understands, no one who seeks God. All have turned away" (Romans 3:10–12 NIV).

- "Christ died for sins once for all, the righteous for the unrighteous, to bring you to God" (1 Peter 3:18 NIV)

The Gospel Is Unlike Any Other

- Not: I obey, therefore I am accepted.

- But: I am accepted, therefore I obey.[1]

"It is by God's grace that you have been saved through faith. It is not the result of your own efforts, but God's gift, so that no one can boast about it" (Ephesians 2:8–9 GNT).

How Do I Become a Christian?

- You must have faith in Christ alone for what He has done on your behalf

"This righteousness from God comes through faith in Jesus Christ to all who believe" (Romans 3:22 NIV).

"If righteousness comes through the Law, then Christ died for nothing" (Galatians 2:21 HCSB).

- You must repent (or turn away) of your sins

"I preached that they should repent and turn to God and prove their repentance by their deeds" (Acts 26:20 NIV).

"And He Himself bore our sins in His body on the cross, so that we might die to sin and live to righteousness; for by His wounds you were healed" (1 Peter 2:24 NASB).

- You must declare that Christ is the Lord of your life

"If you confess with your mouth, 'Jesus is Lord,' and believe in your heart that God raised Him from the dead, you will be saved" (Romans 10:9 HCSB).

Be Sure to Count the Cost

Jesus said, "For which one of you, when he wants to build a tower, does not first sit down and calculate the cost to see if he has enough to complete it?" (Luke 14:28 NASB).

God is more holy that you can imagine; you are more sinful than you will ever admit.

"Seek the LORD while He may be found; call upon Him while He is near. Let the wicked forsake his way and the unrighteous man his thoughts; and let him return to the LORD, and He will have compassion on him, and to our God, for He will abundantly pardon" (Isaiah 55:6–7 NASB).

How Do You Respond?

- Confess and repent (agree with God about your condition and His plan).
- Receive (ask Christ to enter and rule your life).
- Follow (commit to obey because you are accepted).

NOTES

NOTES

Chapter 1

[1]http://www.lifeway.com/Article/LifeWay-Research-finds-unchurched
-Americans-turned-off-by-church-open-to-Christians

[2]Jim Henderson and Matt Casper, *Jim and Casper Go to Church* (Carol Stream, IL: Tyndale House Publishers, Inc., 2007).

Chapter 2

[1]Henry Blackaby and Claude V. King, *Experiencing God: Knowing and Doing the Will of God* (Nashville: Broadman and Holman Publishers, 2004), 77.
[2]C. S. Lewis, *The Weight of Glory and Other Addresses*, rev. ed. (San Francisco: HarperCollins Publishers, Inc., 1980), 26.

Chapter 3

[1]Michelle Rindels, "Poll: Trust in Organized Religion at Near-Record Low," http://www.beliefnet.com/story/220/story_22078_1.html (accessed December 27, 2007).

Chapter 5

[1]We surveyed people who dropped out of church, but had attended regularly for at least one year in high school.
[2]Rodney Stark, *The Rise of Christianity* (Princeton: Princeton University Press, 1996).
[3]Reported in *Christianity Today*, http://www.christianity today.com/ct/2004/novemberweb-only/11-22-23.0.html (accessed December 27, 2007).

Chapter 6

[1]G. Campbell Morgan, *The Gospel According to John* (Old Tappan, NJ: Fleming H. Revell Company, 1986), 270.

Chapter 7

[1]In Philippians 2:5, Scripture points us to what many consider the height of theology in the New Testament. It describes what theologians call the "kenosis." Jesus empties Himself of the outward manifestation of certain attributes, such as His omnipresence, omnipotence, and omniscience.

Chapter 9

[1]LifeWay Christian Resources, "LifeWay Research Uncovers Reasons 18 to 22 Year Olds Drop Out of Church," http://www.lifeway.com/lwc/article_main_pa ge/%2C1703%2CA%25253D165949%252526M%25253D200906%2C00 .html? (accessed December 27, 2007).

[2]James Emery White, *Serious Times: Making Your Life Matter in an Urgent Day* (Downers Grove, IL: InterVarsity Press, 2004), 135.

[3]Ibid.

[4]Timothy George, Galatians: *The New American Commentary* (Nashville: Broadman and Holman Publishers, 1994), 307.

[5]F. F. Bruce, *The Epistle to the Galatians: The New International Greek Testament Commentary* (Grand Rapids: William B. Eerdmans Publishing Company, 1982), 197.

[6]John R. W. Stott, *The Message of Ephesians: God's New Society* (Downers Grove, IL: InterVarsity Press, 1986), 40.

[7]Ralph P. Martin, *The Family and the Fellowship: New Testament Images of the Church* (Eugene, OR: Wipf and Stock Publishers, 1997), 123.

[8]John Calvin, *The Gospel According to St. John 1-10: Calvin's Commentaries*, trans. T. H. L. Parker (Grand Rapids: William B. Eerdmans Publishing Company, 1959), 260.

Chapter 12

[1]Taken from Mark Driscoll's personal study notes on Jonah.
[2]Eugene Peterson, *Under the Unpredictable Plant* (Grand Rapids: William. B. Eerdmans Publishing, 1992), 161.
[3]Ibid., 161.

Conclusion

[1]The song was written by Felice and Boudleaux Bryant, who are buried in Nashville, where I now live. The song, interestingly, was sung by a band called Nazareth, named after the city in Pennsylvania, not the city where Jesus lived. (They also wrote "Rocky Top," the unofficial fight song for the University of Tennessee Volunteers.)

Appendix

[1]We find this phrase helpful and thank Tim Keller for it!

Additional Resources
on Missional Living

Beyond Me
*Living a You-First Life in a
Me-First World*
Kathi Macias
ISBN-13: 978-1-59669-220-6
N084143 • $12.99

Live Sent
You Are a Letter
Jason C. Dukes
ISBN-13: 978-1-59669-315-9
N114149 • $14.99

Faces in the Crowd
*Reaching Your International
Neighbor for Christ*
Donna S. Thomas
ISBN-13: 978-1-59669-205-3
N084131 • $12.99

Available in bookstores everywhere.
For information about these books
or any New Hope product,
visit newhopedigital.com.

New Hope® Publishers is a division of WMU®, an international
organization that challenges Christian believers to understand
and be radically involved in God's mission.
For more information about WMU, go to: wmu.com.
More information about New Hope books can be found at
newhopedigital.com.
New Hope books may be purchased at your local bookstore.

Use the QR reader on your
smartphone to visit us online at
newhopedigital.com

If you've been blessed by this book, we would like to hear your story.
The publisher and author welcome your comments and
suggestions at: newhopereader@wmu.org.